T0122030

Mama's Blessings

Edith Byrd Summerford

WestBow
PRESS
A DIVISION OF THOMAS NELSON

WestBow Press books may be ordered through booksellers or by contacting:

WestBow Press
A Division of Thomas Nelson
1663 Liberty Drive
Bloomington, IN 47403
www.westbowpress.com
1-(866) 928-1240

Because of the dynamic nature of the Internet, any web addresses or links contained in
this book may have changed since publication and may no longer be valid. The views
expressed in this work are solely those of the author and do not necessarily reflect the
views of the publisher, and the publisher hereby disclaims any responsibility for them.

Any people depicted in stock imagery provided by Thinkstock are models,
and such images are being used for illustrative purposes only.

Certain stock imagery © Thinkstock.

ISBN: 978-1-4497-5829-5 (sc)

Library of Congress Control Number: 2012912173

Printed in the United States of America

WestBow Press rev. date: 08/13/2012

In the memory of Mike and Bonnie

Forward

WHEN I FIRST MET EDITH Summerford, while preaching a revival for Pastor Charles Sparks in Hartselle, Alabama, I knew she was different. I met Mike and Bonnie Summerford, Edith's two adult children, while eating with them in their home. They are disabled, and their mother has cared for them most of their adult life.

Edith's difficult and challenging task of caring for her children does not define her; rather, they have been a blessing to her. Thus, MAMA'S BLESSINGS, is a tribute to her precious children who have been an inspiration to her. She found strength to carry on under pressure, and to find joy in trials.

God's grace is manifest in Edith's life as she learned the wonder of God's will for her children. Mike and Bonnie have truly been their Mama's Blessing.

I highly recommend this book for all ages. It is a book you will not want to put down. May MAMA'S BLESSINGS, be read by someone who will realize their need for salvation through the Lord Jesus Christ.

Evangelist Jimmie M. Clark
Lexington, North Carolina

Acknowledgements

I GIVE MY SINCERE THANKS TO all of the following:

- Brother Jimmie M. Clark for prompting me to write a book about my life.
- Dr. Gandhi and staff, for the years they were so good to Mike and Bonnie. For working with me while they were their patients.
- Dr. Vora and staff for the kindness shown during the passing of Mike.
- The doctors and nurses at Hartselle Hospital for the care that was given to Mike and Bonnie all the times they were in the hospital, over the years.
- To the cafeteria for the good food that was brought to me each time they were in the hospital.
- To Hart, Medic-One, then Lifecare Ambulances for the good care given to them when they were transported to the dentist or to the emergency room.
- Dental Associates of North Alabama, to the dentists and staff for all the patience, care and being so good to Mike and Bonnie.
- Morgan County Home Health Nurses and bath girls, for the many years they came to bathe them, the care and the concern they showed.
- Tender Touch, then Oxford for the girls that came to help and take care of Mike and Bonnie.

- My church families, at Bible Baptist, for their many years of prayer, help, love, and the ladies (some husbands) that stayed with Mike and Bonnie for me to go to church.
- Danville Baptist for the things they have done for our family over the years. Brother Jack and June for the kind things done during their passing.
- The late Brother Ted and also Joyce Agee for the many visits and the special things they did for us over the years.
- Phillips Accounting and Tax Service for the help and kindness shown over the years.
- Their Uncle Carl and Aunt Hazel Taylor and Cousin Kathy Irwin, for their visits and love for Michael and Bonnie. Thank you for not forgetting them, after their dad passed away.
- The kindness and love shown by Coy's family during the passing of Michael and Bonnie.
- My special friends, for their love, support and all the things they have done for me.
- Especially my family, for their love, things they did and being there for me when I needed them. I appreciate it from the bottom of my heart.
- My great niece, Nona Livingston for typing my book.

God bless all of you,
I love you,
Edith Byrd Summerford

Introduction

*T*HIS BOOK HAS BEEN WRITTEN to try to be a help to others.

If you have accepted Christ as your personal Savior, there is a mansion waiting for you when you get to heaven. When death comes to a loved one, it hurts so badly, but you can make it. You can survive. It is hard, but it is so much easier if you have the Lord in your life.

I'm just human, too. There were times that I thought I'd not make it another day; because it hurt so badly when Mike passed away, but at least I still had Bonnie. Of course one child cannot replace the other. But, you see life still goes on and Bonnie had to be taken care of.

After Bonnie passed away, I just wanted to go to bed and pull the covers over my head and stay there. Instead of doing that, I did a lot of praying and working. It helps to stay busy, and you can pray while you're working. The Bible tells us to "pray without ceasing" (King James Version 1611, I Thess. 5:17).

The things I have written about my life and the lives of my children are not to dishonor Coy, my ex-husband (whom passed away in November of 1999), but to let others know that when they accept Christ as their personal Savior they are to live their life for the Lord and to do His will.

You see, Coy said that God had called him to preach. He preached a few times and he had a great testimony. After three years and nine months of living for the Lord he let the devil come into his life by consuming alcohol and later alcohol and drugs. He lost his testimony, never to regain it again.

Do I think alcohol should be sold and made legal to do so? No, alcohol and drugs both are tools of the devil. You will do things under the influence of these that you wouldn't ordinarily do.

I pray that this book would be an inspiration and testimony to all who read it, giving our Heavenly Father the glory.

God bless you,
Edith Byrd Summerford

*J*ANUARY 2, 1943 BEGAN THE journey of my life. I came from a very poor family. We share cropped for a living, clearing very little money after paying for the seed and fertilizer.

I can remember getting a new coat once, boy I was thrilled to death. Other than that we wore hand me downs or the clothes mother made for us. But, they were always starched and ironed.

Money was very scarce in our household. Although I do remember, there were times when I was five years old that my brother Frank and my sister Madeline and I would go to the movies. It was called "The Strand" and it was on Main Street in Hartselle. We would go on Saturday to see either Roy Rogers or Gene Autry. Those were movies that we need to have now. There were some good western movies.

After the movie was over, we would go across the street to Elmore's (which use to be called a Ten Cent Store) and get us an ice cream cone. Those were the days! Then, kids could go down the street by themselves and not have to be worried about being kidnapped. I guess that was probably the happiest times that I could remember when I was real young.

Also, when I was about five, I remember my daddy putting a board across a stump. The board had a real long bolt in the center. It was similar to a see-saw except instead of going up and down it went around and around. When you got off, you could hardly stand up. It was called a Flying Jenny. We spent many hours playing on it.

My sister and I would make a playhouse outside by raking the straw and clearing a place out for our rooms. Oh, the fun we would have. Kids nowadays don't know what a playhouse is. It is computer games and all that stuff that I know nothing about. Some never go outside in the sunshine and get fresh air. I remember that my sister and I got dolls once. They were from my older brother Richard; boy did we treasure those dolls.

There were eight kids in our family – four boys and four girls. I was the last little Byrd to be born. I have always heard that the baby gets all the petting. There was no petting in our family.

I never remember my daddy ever telling any of us that he loved us. Although we knew he did, it wasn't ever said around our house. The only affectionate word that daddy ever said to me was when he called me Sister.

My mother showed us some affection, but I think that my mother and daddy were both brought up at a time when parents didn't show affection toward their kids. I'm sure one reason was they worked so hard, especially my mother. I think she was so tired, because her work was never done.

When we moved to the Reeves House my brother, sister, and I would walk to church. Bethel Baptist Church was about a mile and a half from our house.

The shoes we got were very cheap made. I'm sure that they were all our parents could afford. After wearing them awhile, holes would come in the soles. We would cut pasteboard out to put in the bottom of our shoes, to cover the holes. Of course when we wore them awhile or it rained, we would have to replace the pasteboard. We always saved our shoes to wear to school or when we would walk to church. Otherwise, you could find us going barefooted.

My daddy had a problem with his nerves about the time we lived in the Reeves House. I was so young that I didn't realize what was going on. All I remember was that we had to be quiet when we were in the house. He was sick for quite a few months. Then, in January of 1951, we moved to Austinville, to the Manor House.

I was in the second grade of school at the old Austinville Elementary School. I was in Miss Collier's room. That winter there was ice all over the ground, and when we had to go to the bathroom (which was called the outhouse then) we had to go outside. Miss Collier plainly told all of us "Do not skate on the ice." Of course, that was the wrong thing to tell second graders.

Well, you guessed right, I reckon about all of us was punished - a paddling in the open hand with a ruler. Then, we had to stand with our nose in a circle at the blackboard and we had to stand on one foot across the front of the room for awhile. Needless to say, that was the first and last whipping I ever got in school.

After we had moved to Austinville, we made cotton and some sugar cane crops. My brother, sister, and I had to work like adults. We chopped and picked cotton, stripped cane and cut the tops off. If we ever got caught up on all our work, we were not made to go outside and play, we ran like a streak of lightning outside to play. If we didn't daddy or mother one would find another chore for us to do.

Madeline, Frank, and I would go to the big pond that was on the backside of the pasture behind our house. We would go and play in the water, because neither one of us could swim. As we were in the water playing we would see snakes roll off the fence that was on the backside of the pond. We continued to play in the water along with the snakes. Mother would have beaten the daylights out of us if she had known the things we did. You see we were young and didn't know what danger was. The Lord was watching over us.

We would climb up into the barn loft and jump down onto hay, one after another. Never realizing we could have broken an arm, leg, or even our necks. The Lord was watching over us again.

Frank and Tuttle (a friend of his) built a boat and put it into the small pond. Believe it or not it floated, so we would get into it and paddle around on the pond - no life preservers. This pond wasn't as deep though, as the one we played and splashed each other in. There we go with the Lord watching over us again.

When it would get real hot, with no rain, the smaller pond would nearly go dry. We would take our B.B. guns and wade into the water barefooted and shoot snakes. Then, we would catch fish with our bare hands. Of course we thought we killed the snakes, but I'm sure it would just idle them. There we go again with the Lord watching over us.

Our days were spent washing fruit jars and helping mother can fruits and vegetables. We also churned milk with a dasher to make butter. I don't regret having to work hard, because I learned a lot of useful things that has helped me in my adult life. I learned how to survive.

When I was thirteen, I would walk about four miles (from our house to 6th Avenue) and catch the bus that went to Hartselle. I would ride up to the road that went to my sister Lucille's house. I got off the bus and walked about a mile and a half to her house. I would go and help her and her husband work in the fields. By then daddy had quit sharecropping and started working public work. Mother got her a job at the laundry making 35¢ an hour. Yes, you read it right. She brought home about eighteen dollars a week. I enjoyed going to help my sister Lucille and her husband Carl, because I knew they needed the extra help. You see, they only had Carleen and Carolyn and they weren't big enough to help. They were younger than me, so I knew that what extra help they got was greatly appreciated.

Lucille would get up real early and not only cook breakfast, but she would fry potatoes and bake a pan of cornbread for us to take to the field that day. She would take us plates to eat out of. They weren't paper plates because back then we didn't know what a paper plate was. If there were any, we couldn't have been able to afford them. She would take one of the plates and turn it over the bowl of potatoes. The heat from the sun would make the potatoes and cornbread hot. Oh, it was so good.

We always carried a gallon jug of water with us. When we wanted a drink we would take time about drinking out of the same jug. Some people today would say that it was nasty. Well, back then that was the way things were. You didn't go over to the water facet and turn it on. You went to the well and "drawed" it, either with a chain or rope, and it had a bucket on the end of it. You "drawed" a tub of water and let it sit in the sun to warm, if you wanted a bath. We have come a long way. I give God the glory.

We have a lot of modern appliances that we should be so thankful for. Have you thought about not having electricity? When you've lived a hard life, you appreciate it if you have luxuries that come along your way.

I have many fun memories of my school days at Austinville. Our class was like family. At the end of our tenth grade we had to separate. Part went to Danville and the rest of us went to Decatur High for our eleventh grade, except for my friend Anne. She went to Priceville. I had to go to Decatur High because of where I lived. They made an elementary school out of the Austinville High School.

I met Coy (who became my husband later) when I was fourteen years old. He lived down the road from where Lucille, my sister lived. Nell, his sister, and their cousin Lewis Nicholson took us to Rock Springs Baptist Church to hear Junior Hill preach. We started to date a year later. We dated off and on for two years, then, married August 20, 1960.

We were way too young. However, I did have two conciliations, Mike and Bonnie, our children. They were precious gifts from God. Yet at that time I really didn't know who God was. It took many mistakes and a lot of separations for Coy and I before we came to know Christ as our personal Savior.

I remember when Mike was small; he was spoiled because he was the only child for four years. When it was nearly time for Bonnie to be born, I was sitting and concentrating. Coy asked me what was wrong. I told him that I was worried that I wouldn't love this baby as much as I loved Mike. He started laughing and said, "Of course you will." When they put that precious little baby in my arms, I could feel the love rising up in my heart.

Mike and Bonnie had a pretty normal childhood. Mike played baseball on a team in Hartselle that the late Fred Phillips coached. He did a good job playing. He was going to Dr. Crouch at the time and he had him on a diet. So his weight was real good then.

In 1975 we moved to Rock Springs Road right by Mrs. Summerford, my husband's mother. Things were pretty good for awhile. Then, Coy and I started having problems, so he left. We moved our trailer, a month later, behind Brother Jimmy and Joyce Wright's house. Barry, their son, was Mike's friend and Sharon, their daughter was Bonnie's friend. They would get out in the open field, between their house and our trailer, and play softball. Mike would go up to Mike and Sandra Flower's, our neighbor's house, to visit them. Terry Flowers, Mike's brother, would come to see Bonnie awhile, then go home. As soon as he got home the phone would ring, and it would be him calling Bonnie.

Brother Jimmy was pastor at Ironman Baptist Church and Bonnie started going to church with them. She thought she got saved. She went with them to church until we moved in 1980. Coy came back home and in 1980 we bought five acres of land on Old Vaugh Bridge Road.

Bonnie enjoyed mowing for her Grandma Summerford. She also began cooking supper and did a good job. She would have supper ready for us when we got home from work. She worked with me in the summer cleaning up at Miss Conduct.

Mike worked for quite awhile at Danville School in the janitorial department. Mike and Bonnie both got where they couldn't work so they had to quit.

In 1982 we sold our place out on Old Vaugh Bridge Road and rented an apartment on Puckett Road. I really didn't want to move up there, but we didn't have much choice. You know we do what we have to do.

In March of 1983, Bonnie wanted us all to go to church at Ironman Baptist Church – that's what it was called then. Coy and I were really having problems and I didn't want to go, but did because Bonnie wanted us to.

I'll always remember it was the 13th day of March 1983 on a Sunday morning. Mike didn't go with us that morning. We went back again that night. During the alter call Coy and I went forward. I wish I could say that I was gloriously saved, but I had a counterfeit salvation. I just thought I got saved. Coy got saved that night. You see we were encouraged by our daughter, who always enjoyed going to church if she was able to or not – she would go. You could ask her how she felt and she would always say, "Fine."

We were to be baptized the 20th of March, after the evening service. On the morning of the 20th Mike went to church with us. During the invitation the Lord dealt with his heart and he got saved. That night Coy, Mike, and I were all baptized.

It wasn't long after we started to church, we decided to buy a mobile home because Mrs. Summerford was beginning to get sick, and we knew she needed help. So we moved it next to her house.

After we had moved and lived in our mobile home for about four months, we noticed Bonnie more so than Mike, beginning to walk pigeon-toed. It wasn't long after that, she began to fall some.

I thought maybe she was weak in her hips, so I took her to Dr. Payne, the chiropractor. He did adjustments on her for awhile and at first it seemed to help, but then it came to a standstill. Dr. Payne told me he thought she had a neurological problem. He said I needed to take her to a neurologist and he would help me to find one for her.

He recommended Dr. Eston Norwood. I got Bonnie an appointment with him. He did a spinal tap and other tests on her and then wanted her to go to UAB for an MRI. By then Bonnie was walking pigeon-toed all of the time and falling some and dragging her foot.

The MRI showed nothing unusual. Dr. Norwood told us that Mike and Bonnie had a degenerative nerve disorder. That is news that parents don't want to hear. At night I would go out on our porch and cry. One night it was like the Lord was saying to me, "If you want to live to take care of them, you are going to have to take care of yourself." That was the end of me going to the porch to cry. Don't misunderstand me, have I shed tears about Mike and Bonnie since then? You better believe I have – I'm their mother. If they hurt, I hurt.

Mike said in 1985 that God had called him to preach. On December 31, 1985 at our watch night service, Mike preached from Luke 16:19-31. Others preached that night. It has a special memory to me because Brother Donald King came later that night and preached the same scripture that Mike had preached. Hallelujah, nine got saved that night. It was such a blessing.

On March 19, 1986 he preached from Mark 16:1-10. On March 23, 1986 he preached at Oak Ridge Baptist Church for their Youth Day. On October 26, 1986 he preached from Matthew 14:1-3. Mike's preaching career was short lived, but he was such a blessing to me. I was so proud of him. He was having a hard time getting around with his walker.

Although Mike and Bonnie both were using a walker, they never failed to go to church. Bonnie was always up early on Sunday morning, taking her bath when I got up. Mike would then get up and take a shower. Although it was hard for them to get around, they still wanted to go to church.

We were having revival at church in November of 1986. Bonnie was gloriously saved one night after we got home from revival. She was in her room crying, and I asked her what was wrong. She said, "I want to be saved." I called Cindy, my pastor's wife, over and we talked to her and led her to the Lord. Bonnie and I both were convicted of wearing pants during the revival.

December of 1986 would be an event that began to bring about a change that altered the rest of our lives.

Coy went to the concrete place where he had worked before. He owned his own 18-wheeler at that time and was gone quite a lot. I remember it was on Saturday about 5:00 in the afternoon. The phone rang and I answered it. As he began to talk I knew that he had been drinking. My heart sank. He had lived for the Lord, three years and nine months. But see, for a person that has a problem with alcohol cannot go around anyone drinking, unless the Lord sends him. If they do, the devil takes over and the next thing you know you're taking a drink. After that first drink the devil is roughshod over you and it leads to you getting a bottle.

Coy had a testimony and others could see the change in him. Many of his running around buddies watched his life as he went to church. But that day, Coy lost his testimony never to regain it again. We can't play around with the devil without getting burned.

Our life wasn't the same after that. As months went by Mike and Bonnie began to get worse. It would take Mike a good ten minutes to get into the church from the car. He would walk a little ways on his walker, then stand there and rest a minute and then continue doing that until he got into the church. It hurt to watch him struggling. But, Mike and Bonnie didn't give up and stay at home because they had hurdles to cross. They went until both of them couldn't go and that was when they became bedbound.

By 1989 they began to fall a lot. I would have to go home from work and get them up off the floor. As they began to fall more, I had to quit work. Both of them were having hesitation in their speech. Sometimes it would take them a few minutes to say what they wanted too. It never failed that when we had a testimony service at church, they would always ask prayer for their daddy.

Coy wasn't drinking all the time, just every once in a while. So, he would go to church a few times. He never really got back in fellowship with the Lord. He would say he did and the next thing he would be out of church again. We can't play games with the Lord.

In June of 1989 we bought the land next to where we live now on Highway 36. We moved our mobile home there, not knowing what was going to happen eighteen months later.

I began to sell and deliver Avon in January of 1990, when I had someone to stay with Mike and Bonnie. Sometimes JoAnne Flowers, a friend of mine, would come and stay with them for me to deliver the Avon. I didn't realize that when I started selling Avon, how important that it would become to help make a living for Mike, Bonnie, and me.

Mike and Bonnie still were getting worse and us not knowing what was wrong or what they had I couldn't help solve the problem.

As December approached, just before Christmas it began to rain one Saturday morning. Coy was up at Roy's (his brother's house) celebrating Christmas early – the wrong way. It continued to rain all day and looked like it was going to be bad. We wound up getting eighteen inches of rain in a twenty-four hour period before it quit. Coy hadn't come home by 9:00 p.m. that night so Sam and Wayne, friends of ours, went up and brought him home. Coy went to bed as soon as he got home. As it continued to rain I would look outside, but couldn't see anything because it was so dark. Sam would come out every so often and shine his lights back behind the trailer to see how close the water was.

I told Mike and Bonnie to not pull their clothes off because I didn't know when we would have to up and leave. Mike lay across his bed but left his clothes on. Bonnie stayed up with me. I tried to wake Coy up to tell him that we needed to leave. But, he said everything was going to be okay.

As morning approached you could see water fixing to come in the back door of our mobile home. I still tried to tell Coy, but it was to no avail. A little later water began to come in the back door. I heard someone holler. As I opened the front door I looked up toward the highway. Water had washed our front porch away and water was all in the front yard. It was about three and a half feet deep around our trailer. I saw a deputy sheriff on the high side in front of our mobile home. He asked me if we needed help. I said yes that I had a son and daughter that were on walkers. He called the rescue squad and they brought a boat and rescued us. Bonnie was so upset. I know she was scared to death.

The Lord watched over us, because it was a wonder if we weren't electrocuted with the water rising up like it did. Thank you Lord!

When we left the trailer that morning all we had was the clothes on our back and a suitcase with a change of clothes for each one of us. I didn't know where we were going, so we went up to Roy's to stay a few days.

Everybody that was in the flood had to go to the Sparkman Civic Center and the Red Cross helped all of us. They rented us a house on Forest Chapel Road and it was the next Saturday that we moved in. Our brother and sisters from church (it was then called Ironman Baptist Church) brought beds and put them up. Some brought linens, dishes, and food. Hazel and Carl, Coy's sister and her husband, brought a table and four chairs. Some of them brought a refrigerator that Prentis and Betty, from church, loaned us. During the time that they were moving us in, I had to take Bonnie to the emergency room. She could not urinate so they had to catheterize her. The doctor said that her nerves were very upset because of us being in the flood and it got where her kidneys would not act. They gave her a mild sedative to take, to help her. Brenda, from church, went with me to take Bonnie. After we left the emergency room we went back to Roy's to pick up Mike and Coy, and then to go to the house on Forest Chapel Road. Coy was asleep and when I got him awake he said he wasn't ready to go with us. Mike, Bonnie, and I left going to what was going to be our home for the next two months.

As we arrived at the house most of our Christian friends were still there. Thank you Lord, for our Christian friends for all they have done. I don't know what we would do without them.

During the next two months, when I wasn't helping to work on the trailer, I went to check on a loan for us to build on the ten acres we had bought next to the land where our trailer was. Coy and Wayne worked on the trailer during the day and I would go over there at night and work while Coy was with Mike and Bonnie. Brenda came to stay with them while I went to check on the loan. We got a loan from Small Business Association at a low rate of interest.

During January and February we took Mike and Bonnie to UAB and Kirkland Clinic to have tests run. Bonnie already had a skin biopsy and an eye test done. Nothing unusual turned up on Mike or Bonnie's tests.

It was right after Christmas during our ladies prayer meeting on Sunday night that Mrs. Bessie Breeding and Mrs. Ruth Southard presented me with a new Scofield King James Version Bible. Mine was still in the trailer at that time and we couldn't get in because there was water still in there. Wasn't that a blessing for them to think of me?

Finally, after a couple of months of hard work and drying out our trailer we got to move back in. It had plywood floors so that was a plus; we didn't have to replace them. It really looked better when we got done with it than it did when we bought it. We had cut up on the walls to where the insulation was damp and replaced it with new insulation and then put a chair rail above the top of the insulation. It sure was good to be back at home. I think back to the first time I went back inside the trailer after the water subsided. It looked like a tornado had come thru. Things were turned upside down. The refrigerator door had been knocked open and eggs, a ham, and all the other things were all over the place. It seemed like it had been a bad dream, and we were just waking up. It sure looked different now.

As we settled back home Bonnie seemed to be doing better with her nerves.

We got the loan so Coy hired A. D. to frame up the house.

In April, Mike was coming out of their bathroom when he fell forward. I got him up and into his bed. The next morning he complained about his hands hurting. I took him to the emergency room and they x-rayed his hands and said nothing was broken. He didn't say anything about his hip hurting. Mike went from a walker to a bed. Bonnie went from a walker to a wheel chair and then later on to a bed.

By August of 1991 Mike began to get real sick and started running high fever. Their doctor had retired in June of 1991. I started then trying to get a doctor for them. I stayed on the phone for days on end calling different doctors, but all told me that they didn't take Medicaid.

Finally, I contacted North Alabama Regional Council on Government (NARCOG) and they assigned Bertha Berry as Mike and Bonnie's caseworker. She helped me contact the Morgan County Health Department. The Health Department in turn talked to Doctor Michael Putman and he took Mike and Bonnie as his patients. I made the appointment for Mike to go to see him. By then it was the last of October. When Mike went into his examining room, Dr. Putman looked and told me he was going to need surgery. Coy was in South Alabama and couldn't come home because he wasn't in any condition to drive. Sam and Wayne, our friends, went after him. He got back the day before Mike had surgery. At least he was able to be there with Bonnie. So in November of 1991, Dr. Ward did surgery on Mike in his pelvic area. He stayed in the hospital over a week.

Sam and Wayne stayed the first two nights after he had surgery. Mike was in a semi-private room and they wouldn't let me stay overnight with another man in the room with him. Coy couldn't stay because he was going thru his sick spell after coming off of alcohol. I would go stay with Mike during the daytime and be with Bonnie at night. Finally, he got to come home. It was so hard to leave him at night and go home, but I didn't have a choice. I knew Bonnie needed me too. Then, she could still help herself some. I would leave things fixed for her close by and her daddy was there, but most of the time he was in bed. After Mike got home it began a long healing period.

After A.D. got the house all framed up, Coy, Allen, Roy, Mark, Steve, and even Sam was up there working on it. I didn't realize what all was going on besides working on the house. It was about that period of time that I noticed Coy going thru stages of being real mean. I knew he drank every so often, but I didn't realize, till later, that he was also doing drugs.

In February of 1992 we moved into our new house. As we settled in things began to go back to as normal as possible.

In the summer of 1992 Coy was going through a time that he was drinking really badly. Back behind our house was tall sage grass and it was really dry. It hadn't rained for quite awhile. Coy decided to set fire to it. I knew if it got started that it would get the woods and also get up to our house.

I called Brother Steve and Joyce Long, church friends, and told them to start praying that the Lord wouldn't let it catch fire. Well he struck the matches time and time again to start a fire. It would light and burn for maybe three or four feet and then go out. He would try again and the same thing happened again and again. But all you could see was a little trail here and there. Isn't that just like the Lord? Well he got tired of it not burning and just quit and came to the house. There was a prayer answered!

Later on that year I talked with Doctor Putman and he suggested that we take Bonnie to a Doctor Morgan, a neurologist in Huntsville.

We made an appointment and took her to him. He didn't know anymore about her condition than Doctor Norwood did. However, he did make an appointment for Bonnie in Boston, Massachusetts. She would be going to Mass General Hospital. It was a research hospital. The hospital gave me the phone number of a place called The Beacon House. It was a big building with efficiency apartments. I was told that we needed to be there for a few days before they admitted her to the hospital. I wish that I could have taken Mike also, but he was already bedbound and it would have been impossible to do.

By God's grace Ironman Baptist (named then) paid for us to travel by plane round trip to Boston and gave money for us to rent an efficiency apartment and have money, we needed, left over. Isn't that just like the Lord's work?

Linda and Leroy Bunch, friends, were going to stay at the house and take care of Mike while we were gone.

We left on a Wednesday and it was the hardest thing to do, to leave Mike behind. As Bonnie, Madeline (my sister), and I boarded the plane we waved our good-byes to Coy and Bill. The plane ride from Huntsville to Atlanta was a little rough, but the plane was small. Bonnie became nauseated before we arrived in Atlanta.

They had a wheelchair waiting for Bonnie when we arrived in Atlanta and also when we arrived in Boston. The flight to Boston was so much better because the plane was a lot larger and you could feel a lot less turbulence.

As we arrived in Boston they got Bonnie's own wheelchair and we got our luggage. We got a cab and gave him the address for The Beacon House.

When we got to the apartment house we gathered our luggage and got Bonnie out of the cab into her wheelchair. Our apartment was on the second floor. It had a living room/bedroom combination, a kitchen, and a bathroom. The kitchen was tiny, but it served the purpose.

Bonnie had an appointment with a doctor on Friday, so that gave us one day to rest up. We asked about a place close by to buy grocery items and a restaurant near where we were. Madeline and I took time about when we needed to go. We bought coffee and put it in a saucepan and boiled it. The first we made, a spoon would just about have stood up in it, it was so strong. After a few more tries we got where we could make some decent coffee in a saucepan.

We took Bonnie on Friday for the doctor's appointment. He asked questions and then told me he was giving us three jugs to take with us. I was to start that morning when we got back to the apartment, to collect urine for a twenty-four hour period for each jug. It was for a heavy metals test. I collected the urine up until Monday morning. Bonnie had another appointment that morning and Madeline was leaving to go home.

As Bonnie and I got to the hospital they took us to a big conference room. As we entered, all the doctors were there. There were seventeen of them. As I got Bonnie pushed in and took a seat, they began asking all sorts of questions about her. When they were through, they admitted her to the hospital. She stayed in the hospital for eight days. During that eight day period, they did five hundred different tests on her.

The next day is when they began the tests on her. As they became acquainted with Bonnie, the nurses and doctors would want her to talk for them. They liked her Southern drawl.

They would come at all hours during the night to do the tests on her. One reason they did this was because they were trying to get us home by Thanksgiving. As they did test upon test, they couldn't find what was wrong. They said they were going to call it the Summerford's Disease. I was told that they hadn't seen anyone with symptoms like Bonnie had.

Every day I would call home to see how things were going and to talk to Mike. Every time I talked to him, he would say, "Mom, why did you leave me?" Talking about a heartbreaker, it broke mine. By the time I hung up with him it was all I could do to keep from crying. I knew he would be worse if he knew I was crying. Each time I would explain to him that I had taken Bonnie up there trying to find out what was wrong. If they found out what was wrong with her then it would help both of them.

As the tests continued and the days passed, I could tell Bonnie was getting homesick. But, so was I!

Finally, it was the night before we was to go home the next day. One of the doctors came in and asked me if he could do a video of her on his camcorder. I said, "Yes." He said with the video they could compare her to others, which might have the same symptoms, if they came there. Finally, at last we got to go to sleep.

The next morning at 5:30 the nurse came in to give Bonnie a bath. We were to be at the airport at 7:00. An ambulance came to pick us up and to carry us to the airport.

As I got the luggage and her wheelchair checked, it was time to board the plane. All the attendants were very helpful with Bonnie.

When we boarded the plane at Atlanta I could tell Bonnie was worn out from all the tests day and night. We hadn't been in the air over five minutes till Bonnie was sound asleep. I held her head to keep it from tumbling over, all the way to Huntsville. As we arrived in Huntsville, Coy was there to pick us up.

When we got to the house, I couldn't wait to see Mike and get a hung and a kiss from him. But, to my surprise, for at least forty-five minutes he wouldn't have anything to do with me. You see he was mad at me for going off and leaving him. But, it didn't take long after that till I knew he wasn't mad at me anymore. Oh the loving I got then. After we got back from Massachusetts, Bonnie got where she couldn't help me with getting herself in and out of her wheelchair. By January of 1993 she was also bedbound.

The bath girls came from Home Health two days a week to give Mike and Bonnie a bath. On the other days I bathed them. I had a girl thru NARCOG that came three days a week, four hours each day. God is so good to us. He knew it was time that I needed help. He is always on time – never too early or never too late.

Things began to get worse in Coy's and my life. That was when I knew then not only was he drinking, but he was also doing drugs real bad. At that time Mike and Bonnie's mental ability was still good and they realized a lot of things.

By December of 1993 things got so bad that Mike, Bonnie, and I moved to a low rent handicap apartment in town. It wasn't home, but it was quiet and Mike and Bonnie became content there.

Coy started coming around three months later saying that he had quit drinking and he wanted us to come home. I really prayed about it and got peace in my heart about going back.

I told him we would move back home if he would take the sliding doors out at the back and put French doors in. I knew if something happened, if I had to get the kids out, I couldn't push their beds through the sliding doors. The French doors would make it possible for me to get them out of the house.

Coy and Donnie Reeves, a friend, took the sliding doors out and replaced them with French doors. So, after being gone for a little over four months we moved back home. For a month things went okay. Then, everything went back to the way it was before we left. "Lord did

I not listen and follow your leadership," I asked the Lord? But, you see I didn't know what lay ahead of us.

By August everything began to come to a head. Coy and Sam went to check on a truck part and six days later he called and said they were in South Alabama. He didn't even let me know where he was until he finally called. When he called, he told me to go up to my lawyers and go on thru with a divorce that he was moving to South Alabama. He wanted me to pack all of his clothes. I went back to the lawyer and told him to go ahead with a divorce. I had talked to Mrs. Phyllis, our pastor's wife, about it and she said the Lord doesn't want us to be mistreated.

Six days later he was back, staying sometimes at the house and sometimes with his friend. When he got the divorce papers, he wouldn't sign them. He stayed here and there, and then he decided to take me to court to keep me from getting the divorce. Our court day was February 6, 1995 and Judge Glenn Thompson was presiding over our case. He heard each side then he granted me a divorce that day.

You know the Lord gives us strength and faith, but we have to have determination. God has blessed us in so many different ways and the prayers He has answered are numerous.

Coy was to pay the house payment and land payment as long as Mike and Bonnie were alive. In the event of their death it would be sold and divided between Coy and me. After a few months he didn't pay any more land payments and was fixing to be behind in a house payment. He told me that he would sign a quick deed if I would take his name off everything. John Sims, an attorney, fixed up a quick deed, and Coy signed it. So, the payments were mine.

I have always said that was when the Lord gave me extra hours in the day, not only extra hours but extra strength to go with it. The Lord is the only answer to me being able to hold out and work like I was able to. I mowed my yard, sold Avon, started cooking for a living and took care of Mike and Bonnie.

Then, I could mow awhile and go in and check on them. I began baking pies; cakes; cookies; fried peach, apple, and chocolate pies; cinnamon and orange rolls; and sour dough and cinnamon bread. I never advertised, but the Lord blessed us so that I had people calling all the time wanting me to bake something for them. Mid–South Medical Supply called and wanted me to do brown bag lunches for them. I would do anywhere from twenty to fifty lunches a day, one or sometimes two times a week. I did lunches for them about eight months. When Crestline had their Fall Festival that year I baked fifty pies for them.

During that time I thought about selling some of my land because I had ten acres. I knew I would have to put it back into the place. So, in the latter part of 1996 I sold three acres to Craig and Janice Terry. I needed a road, septic tank, and water meter because Coy had connected it all to the other ones that went to the trailer. He sold the land where the trailer was. I knew I was going to need a water meter put in so I had a meter with bigger lines put in. I had Greg White to fix a septic for the house and a 1500 gallon one for two trailer spots. Then, S&S Electric fixed two poles and they were put up. I had to have a road fixed with gravel put on it. Finally, at last everything was ready. In December I rented the first spot to the Woods family.

Later on in September of 1997 I rented the second spot to Henry and Patsy Suggs. The Lord blessed us in such a way that I was able to complete the house on the end with the help of a friend, Anne Shaffer. She got up and measured it and I measured the masonite siding that had to be cut. She got up on the ladder and finished putting it up. The concrete place came and did one side of the carport, because the Hart Ambulance Service had a hard time pushing Mike and Bonnie over the rocks, with the gurney, to get to the ambulance. I told them that one day I would get it fixed so it wouldn't be hard for them to push and it wouldn't be rough on Mike and Bonnie. Years later I was able to have the other side done.

I know many of us have heard the saying and it is in the Bible "ye rejoice with joy unspeakable and full of glory" (King James Version 1611, 1 Pet. 1:8). It was like the Lord had opened the gates of glory for Mike, Bonnie, and me. God gave me the strength and faith to work hard, but He also gave us the increase.

Mike had to have a super pubic catheter put in, in the early part of 1997. It had gotten where his Foley catheter would fill up with bladder stones and stop it up. Dr. Chakrabarty told me he would need a super pubic catheter put in. So, Mike went to Decatur General and the doctor told us if Mike still had stones in his bladder that he would have to blast them to be able for him to pass them. After he did surgery to put in the super pubic catheter he came out and told us that when he got ready to put it in that there was no bladder stones in the bladder. Another prayer answered. Sandra Flowers stayed with Mike that night at the hospital for me to come home to be with Bonnie.

In February of 1997, one Tuesday night, I was cooking to deliver on Wednesday morning and the Lord started dealing with my heart. I knew He was saying to me, "It is time for you to quit cooking." Lord, I know that you know what you're telling me to do, so I'm leaving it in your hands to supply our needs. After I went to bed that night and went to sleep I awoke three times with the Lord telling me that it's time to quit. I will never forget the next day, as I was delivering my pastries, I stopped by Dr. Vora's office and I proceeded to tell them that today would be my last day to sell my pastries. I told them that the Lord said it was time to quit. Ireda, Dr. Vora's nurse, went back and told Dr. Vora and he came up and shook hands with me and said, "Your children are your first priority." He was right, because you see Mike and Bonnie needed me more now because they were getting worse. I finished up on Friday with people saying, "Oh no!" But, I was following the instructions from the Lord. When the Lord closed one door He opens another one.

It was about a week after I quit cooking, when I heard a knock on the door. I went to the door and there was T. C., Wayne, and Mel from church. They wanted to talk to me. They said the church wanted to take us on as a mission at $100 a month. Isn't that a blessing? You see the Lord already had that door open and He was going to see if I was obedient to His word. If I hadn't been, He would have closed that door, maybe never to open it again.

A couple of months after Mike had to have the super pubic catheter put in; Bonnie already was having problems swallowing. This day especially brings back memories. I was having a new central unit installed and Valley Heating and Cooling was where I purchased it. I was going to pay for it through the Joe Wheeler EMC Program.

For some reason they were getting done late. During that time I prepared supper and went in to feed Bonnie first. Neither could use their hands so both had to have someone else to feed them. They could not move their feet either, all they could do was move their head. That day I had prepared hamburger patties, mashed potatoes, and green beans. I cut the meat, which was tender, in tiny-tiny pieces. As Bonnie went to swallow, she began to get choked. I hollered for one of the workers to help me, because I couldn't hold her forward and beat on her back by myself.

The worker came running. I had called Hart Ambulance and before they got there she had quit choking. I called the ambulance service back, and the dispatcher said they were almost at the house so they would come on out and check her to make sure her airway was okay. Thank the Lord it was. The Lord is always on time. Do you think it was a coincidence that it just happened that the workers were late getting done? I don't think so. The Lord knew that I was going to need help.

It wasn't long after that, Bonnie got where she could hardly eat at all and she began to lose weight. She was put in the hospital and they began to give her fluids to build her up. She was on fluids for three days before they did surgery. Dr. Kantamneni put in her feeding tube. She had just about got where she couldn't talk at all. I would say little rhythms and let her finish, so it would keep her brain more alert. Mrs. Phyllis stayed with us that first night.

It wasn't long after that, I was in the kitchen and Bonnie began crying real hard. I went running to see what was wrong. I said, "Bonnie, Bonnie what's wrong?" She said, "Mother, mother my brain is gone." You see, she realized she was getting worse. I calmed her down and stayed with her awhile until she was okay. I then went back into the kitchen, and as I got there the tears began to flow. I said, "Lord, why are both of my children sick and bedbound?" Boy did He put me in my place. He was saying in my heart, "Okay, if you could have one well and the other to be sick, which one would you choose?" I haven't asked that question anymore, because I couldn't pick which one to be sick and which one to be well. Both of them have been such a blessing to me. God has bestowed to me two of the most precious jewels there are. One is a Michael jewel and the other is a Bonnie jewel. They are more precious than any diamond or pearl.

Some people will say, "I feel so sorry for you about the kids." You know when I go to bed, I know where they are and if the Lord chooses to take them on, I know where they're going. A lot of people can't say that about their loved ones.

Danville Baptist Church has been so good to us over the years. They gave us one thousand dollars one Christmas. That was such a blessing. Brother Jack and June have given us a hundred dollars, at Christmas, for years. They're just as the old saying goes "good folks with a big heart". The church people came and painted the house, and they bought shutters and put them up. Also, they cut some trees down and pulled some up by the roots. Later after the front porch was built they came and poured a concrete ramp with iron rails and a sidewalk for a long way. Frank and I put up a bathroom door and built a clothes closet in my bedroom. Brother Frank Sharrott and Joe cut out, in Mike and Bonnie's bathroom, a place to put French doors that he bought. He purchased the lumber and he and Joe built my front porch, all except the roof. NARCOG got Christmas in April volunteers to come and put the roof on. The Lord has been so good to us.

Bonnie began to have bladder spasms so bad that she would bear down and push the bulb of her catheter out with it still inflated. At first she would bleed and bleed. The doctor at UAB put her on B&O suppositories which helped for about a year. Then, it got where nothing would help, so I took her to Doctor Chakrabarty. He did surgery on her and put in a super pubic catheter and started her on Ditropan for the spasms. Mike was having spasms too. So, he prescribed Ditropan for him. It was a great medication for the both of them because you couldn't tell if or when they were having a spasm.

Even thru all the turmoil of things happening to Mike and Bonnie their smiles were so precious. The Lord has kept His hand upon them. We have had so many prayers answered. God has sowed many seeds of blessings in our lives.

In 1998 Mike got where he could not swallow. He would chew and chew but he just couldn't swallow. Doctor Windham put in a feeding tube for him to be fed with, like Bonnie. Neither Mike nor Bonnie was to be given anything by mouth because it could choke them. It is such a blessing that God has given man the knowledge to invent things to help people. Many years ago there was no such thing as a feeding tube.

It is by the grace of God that I was given two precious angels to love and take care of. Would I have wanted them to be well and not sick, of course, but that is not what happened. We have to accept things the way they are. Pray that God will give us the strength and faith that we need to handle situations as they arrive. Yes, it hurts to look at Mike and Bonnie, knowing that each day they are getting worse. The Lord has loaned me two precious children. I pray that when I stand before the Lord, when it comes to Mike and Bonnie, that He will say, "Well done my good and faithful servant." I love them with all my heart. They are my life.

Michael had a badly swollen place between his private parts and his rectum. I took him to Doctor Vakaria and he said it was a fistula. He said if he did surgery on it, the place would stay damp and it would never heal. I pondered on that a few days. Knock, knock, when will we depend upon the Lord? I called Brother Charles and asked if the men of the church would come and anoint Mike with oil and pray for him, (James 5:14-15). "Is any sick among you? let him call for the elders of the church; and let them pray over him, anointing him with oil in the name of the Lord" (King James Version 1611, Jas. 5:14). "And the prayer of faith shall save the sick, and the Lord shall raise him up; and if he have committed sins, they shall be forgiven him" (King James Version 1611, Jas. 5:14).

Brother David Hicks and a bunch of the men from church came that Saturday and anointed Mike with oil and prayed over him. By Monday, surgery was already done. It looked like the Lord had drilled a hole in the fistula and it was draining. It drained for weeks and then it closed up. You couldn't see where the hole was, there wasn't even a scar. Is that not showing a hand of the Lord working? Praise the Lord.

A couple of years ago Mrs. Ester Smith, from church, started coming down to stay with Mike and Bonnie during preaching, where I could go. She made a list and got other ladies to come down to stay for me to be able to go. I was so thankful because I hadn't been able to attend church in two years.

On November 10, 1999, I got a phone call from Coy's niece telling me they had found Coy dead. I had expected something like this, but still you're never prepared. We can't abuse our body with drugs and alcohol and not to expect damage to be done to it.

This was a task that I dreaded doing, but I knew it had to be done. I went into Bonnie's room. As I began to tell her about her daddy her eyes got real big and she began to cry. I comforted her for a while before I went into Mike's room. As I told Mike, his eyes got real big and he began to cry, too. I comforted him also. It broke my heart to see them hurt so. They loved their daddy. Bonnie couldn't talk anymore but Mike could say a few words. It hurt to tell them, but I knew that I wanted to take them one last time to see their daddy here upon this earth. I knew they had to be told.

On visitation day Peck Funeral Home opened up that afternoon for Mike and Bonnie to go to see their daddy. Medic-One and Hart Ambulance carried Mike in one and Bonnie in another ambulance and wouldn't charge me anything. Another blessing!

As they were pushed up to the casket to see him, oh the tears they shed. It would break your heart to see them. You see they realized their daddy was dead. We kept them in their a few minutes for them to see Coy. I didn't take them to the funeral because I knew it would upset them too much - although both ambulance services offered to take them at no charge. I did appreciate it so very much.

For awhile after Coy died I was really mad at him. "Why didn't you think of Mike and Bonnie instead of yourself?" But, I knew in my heart that was between him and the Lord. I have the good memories of when Coy and I were able to talk and get along good after the divorce. He even went into Mike's room and Bonnie's room and spent time with them.

I can't tell you that there haven't been hard times in our lives, because there have been quite a few. But, you know it makes your faith grow stronger. We know that all we have is made possible by our Lord Jesus Christ.

The smiles that Mike and Bonnie would give me were worth a million dollars. When I would go into their rooms and start talking to them they would just glow. Once when I was talking to Mike (before he got where he couldn't talk) and I said, "Do you love me?" He shook his head no, so sweet and innocent. I knew he was teasing me, so I said, "That's okay I don't love you either." He replied, "Yes you do" and I replied back to him, "No I don't." He said, "Yes you do, because you're my mama." Mike loved to tease, but Bonnie was much quieter than Mike. She whines now, but that is the only way that she has to communicate. If people would ask her (after she got real sick) how are you? She would always reply, "Fine." It didn't matter how sick she was.

In 2000, Bonnie was running fever and she was whining different. I knew she was real sick because of the whining she was doing. I could just about tell by each whining she did. I called the ambulance and they took her to the emergency room. She had a kidney infection and she had to be hospitalized. While she was in the emergency room Dr. Benson did a sonogram on her stomach. He said she had gall stones. She was in the hospital for a week and taking IV'S's until she was rid of the infection. Dr. Vakara sent her home after the week was up. She continued to feel bad for at least a month after she got out of the hospital. I went up to Dr. Vakara's office and showed him where I had charted on the calendar where she had been running fever. He hadn't called me about her having surgery on her gall bladder. He got on the phone while I was in his office and set up the date with the surgeon for her to have surgery.

She did real well during the surgery, but she became nauseated when they gave her some pain medicine. They kept her overnight to make sure she was okay. If she needed anything for pain, I would give her Tylenol.

I tried to provide for Mike and Bonnie and I wanted them to be happy. To make it where they would have as normal a life as possible –

even being bedbound. Oh, the tenderness in their eyes when I would go into their rooms.

I regret for Coy the time that he missed, that he could have spent with Mike and Bonnie. The smile that Mike has would melt your heart. Bonnie can't talk so she whines to express herself, like I said I recognize her different whines.

If a commercial or a program comes on she doesn't want to watch, she will let you know immediately. Oh, but the loving I get early in the morning is worth it all and such a blessing. When she is done with giving me loving she wanted me to go on and leave her alone. Mike on the other hand would be content to have me to stay in his room all day long. I could point to my cheek and say, "Give mama loving." He will open his mouth a little and I will put my cheek up to him that is his way of giving me loving. When the ambulance would come after Bonnie to take her to the dentist or the emergency room she would pick out which one looked the best and she would smile at him.

Mike would smile with his winning smile and the nurses would tease him and tell him that he was flirting with them. He liked that.

I wouldn't trade my son and daughter, like they are, for well ones. I would love for them to be well, but they're not. They have brought me so much joy in my life. The Lord knew what I needed in my life for it to be complete.

I have never asked for patience. I remember what Mrs. Joyce said when she said to Brother Steve about praying for patience. Brother Steve told her to always remember Job. The Lord has given me patience.

My brother gave me a small mobile home. I put it on the back lot of my rental spots. Brother Wendell came over and I helped him to hang sheet rock on the two bedrooms. Doyle Collins and I put paneling in the living room and built a cabinet for the sink in the bathroom. I worked on the trailer while the caregiver, Glenda Baggett and later Crystal Campbell sat with Mike and Bonnie. I painted the kitchen, bathroom, hallway, and the two bedrooms. I rerouted the drain line from the kitchen sink to the line that went to the septic tank. I also underpinned the trailer with galvalon. What I didn't know how to do I would ask someone. After the carpet and linoleum was down, I gave it a good scrubbing and rented it out for three years, and then I sold it.

The Lord has been so good to Mike, Bonnie, and me. The many prayers and all the blessings that the Lord has bestowed upon us are unspeakable.

Once I had to purchase a battery. A few days later I was going to go through my coupon package, but changed my mind and started to throw it aside, to do it later. But I thought, well I'll get out the ones that had expired and throw them away. Well, I unzipped it and low and behold, guess what; there were twenty-five one dollar bills inside. Did I put them in there? You would think if I did I would surely remember it. Did the Lord place them there? Miracles do happen, even today. I think when we start talking about miracles, it scares some people.

On April 8, 2004 just before 3:30 am, I was awakening from a deep sleep, gasping, thinking that I was dying. I couldn't breathe. I jumped up out of bed, got down on my knees and started praying.

While I was praying, I could feel in my heart, the Lord saying to me, "Edith, if you died right now would you go to Heaven?"

I couldn't answer yes to that. Boy, I was scared to death. I went to the kitchen table, got my Bible and started reading it.

I knew how to go about leading myself to the Lord. I confessed I was a sinner, and that Christ was the son of God. He died on the Cross for my sins and arose the third day. His blood covered our sins as far as the east is from the west to be remembered no more. Even after doing all that, I still stayed at that kitchen table and continued to read until 5:30 that morning.

It felt like a load had been lifted off my shoulders. I was a sinner saved by grace through faith. I had taken off that old coat and put on a new one.

In August of 2004, Mike became real sick and had to be hospitalized for a kidney infection. The doctors and all the nurses at Hartselle Hospital have always been so nice and good to Mike and Bonnie, whenever they were in the hospital. They were always good to me also. It always made the stay easier. Glenda Ferguson from Home Health stayed one night with Mike and I went home and stayed with Bonnie that night. I never left them alone while they were in the hospital.

Patsy, my neighbor, would stay at home with the other one while I was at the hospital. If I had to leave the hospital to go to get my medicine, to pay bills or to do anything else Marie, a friend from church, would come up and stay. Hazel stayed once and Mrs. Phyllis stayed once. I was so grateful that they were able to come and stay. It wasn't too long after Mike had gotten home from the hospital that the Lord did surgery on him again. It looked like the Lord had bored a hole in the fistula again. No tears or ragged edges, just a smooth round hole. It drained again for about three weeks and just as quick, it closed up, with no scar. That's just like the Lord. He gave the birds' knowledge to round out their little nest so even, all the way around. Boy, don't miracles happen in this day and age. The breath that we breathe, the warm sunshine, the beautiful flowers and even most of all the opportunity to have the chance to accept the Lord Jesus Christ is a miracle in itself.

I began to have some female problems and Dr. Crouch sent me to Dr. Ray. Dr. Ray told me I needed a complete hysterectomy. He made my appointment for surgery in November of 2004. It broke my heart to have to leave Mike and Bonnie for three days to have surgery. I knew I didn't have a choice. I was to go thru the emergency room and to be down there at 12:01 am to be admitted. Madeline came by and got me. After they admitted me and I got into my room, Madeline made her bed in the recliner that made into a bed and went to sleep about 3:00 a.m. I never went to sleep, just catnapped and at 6:00 they came to take me to surgery. The surgery went well, but I was really nauseated when I got back to my room. I put a wet cloth across my throat to keep me from getting sick. Later that day I called to check on Mike and Bonnie. They were doing fine, but I missed them so.

My brother, Fletcher came to set with me that night after I had surgery. After he had stayed awhile I told him to go on home, because I knew he had to go to work the next day. I sure appreciated him being there. My stomach hurt so badly from gas and I couldn't get rid of it. The nurse gave me some medicine for gas, but it didn't do any good. Finally, at last I went to sleep. The next day my stomach was still hurting. The nurse told me if I would walk that it would help. I think I walked so much that if you looked real hard – part of the carpet would have looked worn. I still didn't get rid of it.

I would call and check on Mike and Bonnie, and then I would walk. Finally, at last it was time for me to go home. Madeline came after me and drove me home. We stopped at Kroger's to get my prescription filled. When we got home, I don't know who was the most proud to see each other, me or Mike and Bonnie. You see I would always pray at bedtime with them. Later the Lord dealt with me about praying each time I fed them. He let me know that it was their mealtime too. So I began to pray each time that I fed them or gave them their medication.

Madeline stayed with me the first night after I got home. Patsy stayed with Mike and Bonnie while I was in the hospital. When I got home she stayed the night after Madeline stayed and for about three weeks at night and came to turn Mike and Bonnie during the day. She has really been a big help to me.

Bonnie has started to cry more when I would start to leave. I always kiss them bye before I leave. She realizes that I am going and she is not getting to go with me. I decided then that I would give her a good-bye kiss a while before I left. That way she wouldn't realize that I had gone.

The nurses always called Mike the Flirter. When he could wink, he would wink at them. He went from that to a whistle, which he couldn't blow out so he sucked in his breath to whistle. You could tell when he was getting worse. Both of the children went through different stages. After that he went to making a clicking sound out of the side of his mouth with his teeth and tongue. It was a similar sound you would make to get a horse to giddy up. After that he would give his sweet smile, later on as he got real bad it was hard for him to even smile.

In September of 2005, rain came in at the French doors in the back, ruining the doors and my rug in the dining room. Frank told me, before I replaced my doors and rug, that I needed a porch with a roof to keep the rain from coming in on them.

So we began to get started. My balance was bad, when my left knee was swollen. I had been going to Dr. Sharpe. I was told I needed a knee replacement. I was waiting on approval from the insurance company for surgery.

We put the lumber out at the back where the porch was to be built. As I turned around I lost my balance and sat right down on a 2x8 that was turned up sideways. It hurt so bad as I tried to get up. I knew when I got up that I had hurt my tailbone. I went in and called Dr. Crouch, but they were on vacation. So, I called Dr. Vora. Gerri, the receptionist said they could see me. So I went in and took a bath.

Dr. Vora sent me in for x-rays. As I went and sat down in his office, he began to tell me that my tailbone was badly bruised. He said it would take time for it to heal.

In October I got the approval to have my surgery done, but I told them I wanted to wait until November. I knew by then my tailbone should be better.

Needless to say Frank and I built the porch. We started on the floor. Doyle and Margie Collins, friends, came over and finished the rest of the floor. Isn't it a blessing to have family and friends to pitch in and show their love?

T. C. and Marie came by and got me the morning I was to have surgery. I think we got to the hospital at 5:00 a.m. When we got there, low and behold if Anne wasn't already there waiting on us.

The surgery went good. I remember the nurse telling me, when they had me back in my room, to breathe deeply. I began to get nauseated and I had to put a wet cloth across my neck. My tailbone hurt worse than the knee replacement. I couldn't eat because I felt sick to my stomach. I knew it was the Morphine, but I hadn't been mashing the pump. Dr. Crouch told the nurses if I needed anything for pain to give it to me by mouth.

On Thursday, Dr. Sharpe came in and told me my blood was low and I needed two pints or units. They started giving it to me about 5:00 p.m. When I had half of the pint gone, I began to get hungry. The nurse brought me some crackers and I ate every one of them. I hadn't eaten anything but drank some tea and broth.

Oh how I missed Mike and Bonnie. I would call about them and Patsy would hold the phone to their ear and I would talk to them. Crystal stayed during the day and Patsy would stay at night. After I came home, Patsy stayed with us at night. After a couple of weeks she would only come when they needed turning and I would feed them. I would put their platter in the wheelchair and push it in to feed them.

Marie took me to therapy three times a week. Mrs. Phyllis took me once and Anne took me one time. Five months after I had surgery, Dr. Sharpe said I had scar tissue so I had to have surgery again. This time he did it at the Surgery Center. I think it hurt more than the knee replacement. So it was to therapy again. Bless her heart, Marie took me again. I sure have been blessed to have friends so dear. After going to therapy so much, when it was through it was like being let out of a cage.

I sure missed not getting to go to church. There were a few preachers that I would watch. Charles Stanley, David Jeremiah, and John Hagee were the few preachers that I think preached the gospel. Even though I like listening to them it was not like being in our own church, listening to God's man bringing us the message. I don't understand a child of God not wanting to be in church when the church doors are open.

Well, finally at last I'm well enough to drive myself to church. I still have to use a walker for awhile, but at least I can go. Praise the Lord. It seems like the days just fly by.

Here it is December of 2006. Mike and Bonnie both have a bad habit of biting their toothbrushes. Bonnie uses about ten to twelve in a month. Sometimes a toothbrush will last one time. Mike is not as bad as Bonnie, but he still likes to bite it. It was just before Christmas on a Saturday night. I was brushing Bonnie's teeth on the side and was fixing to take the tooth brush out. All at once she bit down and I knew without looking she had broken her teeth. Sure enough, the front tooth and the one next to it had the bottom half broken off.

On Monday morning I called Dr. Hawkin's office. Hannah answered, and I told her what had happened. I don't know if Dr. Greg can fix it or if they will have to be pulled. She told me what time to bring her that day. I called Lifecare for them to pick her up. As we arrived they did x-rays on her teeth. The Lord shined His blessing upon Bonnie that day. Dr. Greg came in and said that her nerve wasn't exposed. He drilled little holes into the root and put pins in them. He then built the lower parts of those two teeth with enamel. It's such a blessing to see doctors use the knowledge that the Lord gives them. I was so thankful he was able to save her teeth; I didn't want her to lose them if he could save them.

We got ready to go and I waited for her to give me the bill, then I asked for it. She told me there was no charge, that it was our Christmas present. Isn't that such a blessing? That's just like the Lord. I was expecting, if he could even fix it, for it to cost $750 to $800. I couldn't help but cry, because it blessed me so much that there are people that really care. Praise the Lord! The kids had a good Christmas. I always decorate their rooms and put the Christmas cards we get around each one of their doors.

Another year has come and gone. Here it is spring again. It is time for me to get out and start me a garden. It sure does cut down on the grocery expenses to have one. I don't have a big one, because I can't get out and work in one too long at a time. You never know if Mike or Bonnie might get sick, and I work in it while Megan is here with them.

Bonnie's allergies are really bothering her. She has begun to get choked. Especially at night it seems to be worse. Susie, the nurse from Home Health, came out on two different occasions and suctioned down in her throat to get the mucus out. Dr. Gandhi put her on Claritin and then on Allegra, neither helped her. There were many nights that I had to jump up every fifteen to twenty minutes and suction her mouth out. Dr. Gandhi then prescribed Zertec for her to take all of the time. It sure has been a life saver.

God uses doctors many times for His healing. He gives them the knowledge to do what they do.

Well, I've canned beans, tomatoes, and squash. I also canned peaches and this spring I put cherries in the freezer to make jelly later.

My garden is gone now. But the yard is still to be mowed quite a few more times before fall sets in. I don't mind mowing unless it's real hot. Then, I'm like a flower, I just wilt.

Well, I started digging the holes for my shed. I would dig a little and then put water in it and then dig some more. It was so dry. I guess you've heard the saying? "It's so dry I could spit cotton." Well, it was about that dry.

I had a pretty good ways dug on them and I think Shirley sent Wendell over to finish them. It was so hot. I sure was proud that they were through. Between Frank, Wendell and Henry helping I didn't have to help a whole lot more. Anyway, I only got to work while Meghan was here. Well the shed is finished. It looks right nice. I don't think we can have too many outside buildings. They sure come in handy.

Well Christmas won't be long off, so it's time to decorate. I always put a tree in each of their rooms. It is just a small optic tree that I set on the table.

Sometimes they will just look at it. It makes me wonder at times what they are thinking. You know it breaks my heart because their noses could be itching and I wouldn't even know it. I have seen times that their eyes have been red. I would look into their eyes and they would have a hair or sometimes more than one hair in their eye. I would get it out and then put eye drops in them. Do we not have a lot to be thankful for, if we have good health? We should be on our knees thanking God. If we can't get on our knees we should have a prayer in our heart and on our lips.

I have a friend, Shirley Singleton that has been a friend to me for fifty years. She has a son that is afflicted. He is a blessing to her and not only to her but everybody else. His name is Tim and he loves watches. When I call over there, he will ask me when I get my mail out of the box or when I put my garbage out. He tells me that he watches Channel 19.

Can't you see the hand of the Lord in ways that he works? You see, Tim wasn't supposed to live beyond an early age. He is forty-five years old. Shirley and I have spent many times talking on the phone. Her husband Robert passed away in January of 1988 with cancer. She has been a blessing to me over the years. Neither of us gets out much, so it is a help to have someone in a similar condition to talk to.

Marie Garrett, Anne Shaffer, and I talk quite a bit. They are also friends of mine. Anne and I met when we were eight years old. We have

32

been good friends every since then. Marie and I met in 1960 when I went to work at the uniform place. I quit there in 1965 before Bonnie was born. I didn't see her again until she and T.C. came visiting at church in 1990. It sure is good to have friends you know loves the Lord and lives for Him.

Well 2008 is here and thank you Lord that we're alive. This year has started out pretty good.

Bonnie seems to have lost some weight. We've increased her feeding an ounce. It will take a while before you can tell any increase in her weight. We can't give her too much because it causes her to have a lot of gas and she can't get rid of it.

In March I noticed a small red spot on the top of her bottom when I turned her over. I knew with her losing weight, that it could develop into a bad situation, so I had to keep an eye on it. I began to put Lantiseptic cream on it. Susie, the Home Health nurse, put a DuoDERM bandage on it. It was in a bad place so it had to be changed often to keep it clean.

Jean Johnson, my next door neighbor who became a good friend, came over and we were talking. She asked me if I thought a flotation mattress would be of any help to Bonnie. I said, "You don't know what a blessing that would be." Jean had taken care of her sister a few years before. She was bedbound and had to have a flotation mattress. Her sister had passed away and someone else had borrowed it, but they didn't need it anymore. So Dick and Jean went to Kentucky and brought the mattress back.

We cleaned it up and put it on Bonnie's bed. Four days later the red spot was gone. Do I think that it was a coincidence that Dick and Jean bought the house next door and moved in? No, I don't think so. I believe it was the hand of God working. See, Dick and Jean's grandson, Adam, was really bad off and they came from Kentucky to help with him – he passed away in January of 2010. He lived at Hazelgreen. Yes, I said Hazelgreen. How did they get next door to me from Hazelgreen? I believe the Lord guided them in this direction. Do I think it was a coincidence that Bonnie needed the mattress now instead of a year ago or two years ago? No, the Lord is always on time – never too early, never too late.

Always remember John 11:43-44 when Jesus cried out with a loud voice "Lazarus, come forth" (King James Version 1611, John 11:43). "And he that was dead came forth, bound hand and foot with graveclothes: and his face was bound about with a napkin" (King James Version 1611, John 11:44). Jesus saith unto them, "Loose him, and let him go" (King James Version 1611, John 11:44). That makes me want to have a shouting fit. Do I think that the miracles were just in the Bible, no I've seen too many happen in our lives?

I've noticed there's a change in Mike. He will smile but it takes a lot longer to get him to. He just seems like he doesn't have the strength. He doesn't watch TV as much as he did. He has begun to look into the living room up toward the ceiling. He will just stare like he's looking, but not really seeing anything.

Mike and Bonnie haven't felt good for awhile. Bonnie's temperature has been averaging about 100° and Mike's has been running low at an average of 95.4°. He also had some blood signs in his urine. Susie came out to take a urine specimen of Mike and Bonnie. When we got the results back, they had to be put in the hospital to be given medication by IV. I asked Sandra, Dr. Gandhi's receptionist, to see if they could be put in the same room. We can always pull the curtain if we need too. She said she didn't think that would be a problem. On November 3, 2008 they were admitted. That day began another major change in our life.

After they were admitted, Dr. Gandhi came by late that afternoon. He checked their lungs and listened to their heart. He asked for a chest x-ray to be done on Mike. It showed that he had fluid in his right lung, so they started him on Lasixs. After blood work was done the doctor put both on tobramycin and Zosyn. Bonnie was also put on vancomycin.

Mike began to take thyroid medicine. Dr. Gandhi said that his thyroids were inactive and his sodium was low so he started talking one teaspoon of salt a day. Mike had been running 95.4° since July of this year. The doctor said it was because of his thyroids.

Dr. Gandhi asked me when he came in to check them, if they could understand things. I told him that Bonnie did some, but Mike could understand more. He said when he was through examining them he wanted to talk to me in the hallway. I knew by what he said that the talk was going to be serious.

When he was through, we went to the hallway. He asked me if any doctor had ever told me what was wrong with Mike and Bonnie. I told him all I was ever told was that it was a degenerative nerve disorder. He told me they had muscular dystrophy. He then asked me if I had thought about life support. I told him no. He began to tell me that the disease would start at their kidneys and go up. He said I needed to think about it.

Bonnie had a growth on her private part. I had talked to the nurse about it and said I didn't want anything done until it had to be. Now it had gotten to the point that something needed to be done. While we were in the hospital Dr. Gandhi told Dr. Roberts and he came by to take a look at it. After he looked at it he said he would be right back. It wasn't long till he came back and I noticed he had a string in this hand. He said Bonnie was in no condition to have surgery. He had talked to Dr. Gandhi and he said he told him what he wanted to do and he wanted to run it by me to see what I thought. He wanted to tie the string around the growth to cut the flow of blood and said it would fall off. I told him to go ahead – I was in total agreement. He called the nurse in. She held one leg and I held the other while he tied the string.

I appreciated Dr. Roberts being concerned about Bonnie's condition. He used good common sense. It fell off in five days.

Mike and Bonnie had been in the hospital seven days and Bonnie's temperature was still nearly 103°. They couldn't figure why her temperature didn't go down with her taking all three antibiotics by IV. But, on the seventh day of their stay we saw another one of God's miracles take place. That night, just before 6:00, I had turned Bonnie over to check her bottom to make sure it was clean. Patsy the R.N saw a spot on her bottom and asked me about it. I told her it had been there since she was born. As I went to put her on her back, I saw something between her legs. The first thought that came to me was that the antibiotics had caused her to have diarrhea. As I turned her back over on her side where I could check her, I pulled on her draw sheet and put a little pressure on her hip where it would steady her and she wouldn't tumble over. As I applied the little pressure the spot we were talking about burst loose and corruption started pouring out. I mashed the button for the nurse. She came running, then she saw what was going on, so she ran back to get a tube to do a culture. She put some in the tube and sealed it. We mashed and wiped for the longest. She estimated about two cups came out.

I pointed to the three IV'S's connected up to Bonnie and said, "You see all the IV'S's with antibiotics in them? The Lord gives the doctors' knowledge to figure what medications to give her, but it took surgery performed by the Lord to finish the process." You see, Bonnie had a round hole where the place was, not torn nor any ragged edges. That shows the hand of the Lord working.

Dr. Roberts was called in; he said that it was an abscess. He packed it with two feet of medicated iodoform packing. He had measured it and it was three inches deep. I laid my hand on Bonnie and you could tell that her fever had gone down. The abscess had to be packed two times a day so that caused her to have to stay four extra days. They wanted her to have the extra antibiotics. Mike got to go home the tenth day. So Patsy stayed with him.

During this hospital stay, I was able to talk with many of the nurses, lab technicians, cafeteria girls, girls in housekeeping and others about how the Lord has worked in our life. The Lord has been so good to us. The many opportunities the Lord gave to me to be a witness to others, I am so thankful for. Some of us even cried together because they had incidents in their lives too. Joyce Wright, a nurse who worked at the hospital, was always a help to us. She brought the medicine around and made sure Mike and Bonnie's medicine was on time, as near as possible.

When we got home from the hospital, Mike's fever kept staying between 94.6° to 95.8°. He just wasn't himself. We got through Christmas as best as we could.

If anybody would have asked me before November of 2008 which would I thought would pass away first, I would have said, "I think it would be Bonnie." The reason is because she had become so frail. But after November I knew it wasn't going to be Bonnie, that it would be Mike. He had sure gone down fast.

I really prayed and gave much thought to what Dr. Gandhi had discussed with me. A few days later, I talked with Hazel about the decision the Lord had impressed upon my heart. Sometimes we don't want to face things, but we know they have to be done. My children are all I have and I love them with all of my heart and soul.

Here it is the last part of March, Mike and Bonnie aren't feeling good. Susie came out to take a urine specimen. We will hear from the results by the first of the week.

We are having a three day revival with Brother Jimmie M. Clark as the visiting evangelist. So, on March 31, 2009, I invited Brother Charles, Mrs. Phyllis, and Brother Jimmie over for supper. During the meal Brother Jimmie told me he thought I should write a book about the children and me. He then went on further to say he already had a title; you can call it Mama's Blessings. He spoke the truth. They sure have been a blessing.

On April 1st of 2009 we got the results back on the specimens and it was bad enough for them to be hospitalized with IV'S's. Each time we go to the hospital it's like we are moving. There are extra pillows and pillow cases, toothbrushes, toothpaste, pads, medicines, brushes and combs, and you name it. I carry a garbage bag of pillows, a suitcase and a big tote bag. But I know we will be there at least a week and I don't want to forget anything.

Things went a little better this time, but Mike's thyroid medicine had to be increased. His sodium was much lower so he was given two teaspoons of salt a day. Dr. Gandhi checked Bonnie's thyroids which turned out to be low, so he started her on thyroid medicine. She was to continue to take one-half a teaspoon of salt a day.

I can look at Mike and see he is really going down fast. He doesn't smile anymore. Like I said before, he seems to not have the strength. He just stares a lot. It breaks my heart to see him without that big ole smile. He watches me a lot when I am in his room and then he'll stare at the ceiling in the living room.

Well, Mike had his birthday June 30th and Bonnie the 10th of July. I had thought about having a supper and inviting my family. But, I knew Mike and Bonnie weren't up to that, especially Mike. So, they got their gifts on their birthday and I sang "Happy Birthday" to them. I knew Mike was bad, because he didn't have that twinkle in his eyes anymore.

I told Marie, after Mike had his birthday, that he wouldn't see another one. I knew in my heart that he wouldn't. I didn't want to think about it. But, like Brother Wendell said (after Mike had passed away) the Lord was preparing me for what was to come about. Bless you Lord!

About the middle of July I went to the mailbox. As I got the mail out of the box, I noticed an envelope addressed to me. I thought, boy they sure have a beautiful handwriting. I glanced at the return address to see who it was from. It said 3456 Hwy. 36 W., Hartselle, Alabama 35640. Hey, that's my address. Boy that's strange. So I opened the letter and there was $34 inside. Thank you Lord Jesus. Since then, nearly every month, I have gotten a letter with a different amount of money each time. There's always a little note like, "God bless", "Have a good day", or "Thought this might help, God bless". Do I know who is sending these? No, I don't have the slightest idea. But it is such a blessing to receive them.

Two weeks before Mike passed away, Marie and I were talking. I told her that I had a bad, bad feeling about Mike.

On the 6th of September 2009, when I got home from church, Meghan told me that Mike was breathing a little different. I went in to check on him and he was breathing different, not bad just different. I got his humidifier and plugged it up. It seemed to help some. He slept fairly well that night.

The next day, Jean came at 12:00 to stay with Mike and Bonnie. I went out, as soon as she got there, to mow, so I could get done before she had to leave. As I put the mower up and went to wash up, Jean told me Mike's breathing was worse. I went in and checked on him. He was getting worse. I checked on him quite often. As I fed their last feeding with their medicine at 10:00 p.m., I could tell that it wasn't going to be long before we would have to go to the hospital.

As I stood by his bed, he didn't take his eyes off me. I think he knew something bad was wrong. At 11:00 p.m. I called Jean to come stay with Bonnie and then I called the ambulance. I told them he was having a problem with his breathing.

They came out and put oxygen on him. Then, we left the house for the last time, alive for Mike.

When we got to the emergency room at Hartselle, the doctor came right on in to check him. When Dr. Donley was through she stepped out of the room and I went with her. She put her arms around me and told me that she wished there was more that she could do. She said they were sending him to ICCU. I saw Sammi (she went to school with Bonnie) and I asked her about Mike. She said that yes, he was real bad.

Bonnie Faye Summerford

Bonnie at 4 years old

Bonnie in First Grade

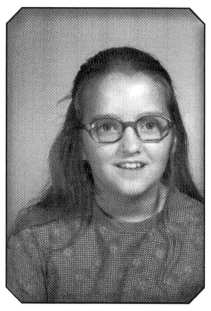

Bonnie at 10 years old

Bonnie at 14 years old

Bonnie at 15 years old

Michael Joe Summerford

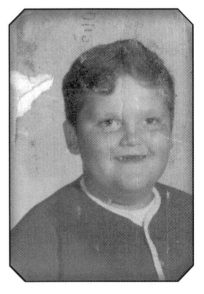

Michael at 7 years old

Michael at 9 years old

Michael at 14 years old

Michael at 15 years old

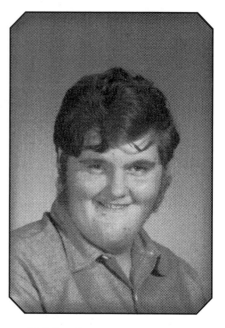

Michael at 16 years old

I CALLED BROTHER CHARLES; HE SAID Mrs. Phyllis was asleep. I called Marie, her and T. C. came right on up to the hospital. Marie stayed all night and part of the next day with me and Mike in ICCU. I think T. C. stayed all night in the waiting room.

Mike was beginning to breathe from his upper chest. They put the C-pap on him instead of just the oxygen.

When Dr. Gandhi came in, he examined him and told me that he was bad. He asked me if I had decided about life support. I told him I didn't want it put on him. I knew that if it was put on him that it would be a repeat of the same thing. I couldn't stand to see him suffer. It's hard to tell a doctor that you don't want life support put on your son, because then, you know what is going to happen. This is my son, my first born, part of my heart, my kids are my life.

"Lord, I don't know how I can make it without Mike." The Lord reminded me of the prayer I had prayed for many, many years. "You ask me to let you live and stay in good health to be able to take care of Mike and Bonnie, I've done that." As the Lord reminded me, I asked, "Lord, please let Mike go easy."

I can't remember who all came on the 8th which was Tuesday. Madeline and Sandra stayed with me that Tuesday night. It was a long, rough night. Madeline left about 5:00 Wednesday morning. Sandra and I would watch Mike's vital signs. They were getting real low.

It was 5:30 a.m. when I looked over at Mike and he opened his eyes. I walked over and started talking to him. "I love you son, you're going to be crossing over soon. Look for Bonnie and me. We won't be far behind you." The nurses came in real quick to see. They said, "His mother is talking to him." You see his vital signs had gone up.

Dr. Gandhi came in around 9:30 and checked Mike. He told me he was really bad. He asked if there were any questions I wanted to ask him. I wanted to know when he thought the time would be. He told me it would be today. It was like a death sentence, but I already knew in my heart that it wasn't going to be long. He said I could stop anything that I didn't want done to Mike. All I wanted on him was oxygen. There wasn't any use of doing anymore blood work or any other tests. There was nothing else human hands could do. The Lord would take over now.

The nurses tried to make us as comfortable as they could while we were in the unit with Mike.

Sharon was the R. N. on that shift. She came in to tell me they were moving Mike to the 3rd floor. I knew it wasn't long, but the rest of the family could be with him, also.

It was about 1:15 when they had all the paper work done and the room ready. The nurses rushed him up to the 3rd floor, while one pumped where he could breathe. As they settled him in the room family began to come in. A little later the phone rang, and it was Danny Bruce. I talked to him a few minutes and Allen told me that I needed to be with Mike. Adel and Carolyn were sitting on the other bed so I just gave the phone to Adel.

As I went over to the left side of Mike, I laid his left hand across my right hand. I got real close to him then I began to sing "Jesus Loves Me." I sang the song that I wrote for them when they were in the hospital in 2008. As I was praying heavens doors were opened up and Mike took his flight with angels ushering him home to be with the Lord. But as he was taking that flight he squeezed my hand with his left hand, which he hadn't used in at least 15 years. Oh it was such a blessing to have that memory. I believe in my heart he was saying, "Mom, everything is okay."

The nurses from ICCU, the 2nd floor nurses and the 3rd floor nurses came in — one after another. They each offered words of sympathy, some of them had known the children for years. Mike and Bonnie had been in and out of the hospital at Hartselle for about eleven years.

A few minutes later, Dr. Gandhi came in to pronounce him dead. He said he was sorry and if there was anything they could do. I appreciated his offer of jester, because not many doctors would say that.

A few of us went to the waiting room as they got Mike ready to go to the funeral home. After a little while Peck's Funeral Home came after him. It was hard to watch him go past us. After they got on the elevator with him, we wanted a few minutes and then we left.

Sandra drove me home. She sat in the kitchen with the others. I put my purse up and went to Bonnie's room. I dreaded this, but I knew it had to be done. I put my arms around Bonnie and told her how much I loved her. As I began to tell her about Mike, her eyes got real big as I told her he passed away, she began to cry real hard. I told her he had went home to be with the Lord and that we would join him one day.

Although she couldn't talk or understand some things, she realized that Michael had passed away. I continued to have my arms around her and reassured her we would join him soon.

People began to come in. Some brought food and others came to give their condolences. The phone was a constant ringing instrument. Patsy and a few others wanted to stay that night with Bonnie and me, but I wanted for us to be by ourselves.

We needed that quiet time together for me to be able to talk to Bonnie and to give her special attention. We made it alright, but it was hard because I wanted to go to check on Mike and get him ready for bed also. But, Mike wasn't there; he was in the presence of the Lord.

It is hard to do the regular routine, things that have to be done, when you have such a burden on your heart. But, life does go on, sometimes you would like for it to be at a standstill.

Frank and Sarah came the next morning after Meghan got here. She stayed with Bonnie while we went to the funeral home to make the arrangements. I had a 10:00 a.m. appointment.

When we got to the funeral home, Freddie took some of the information and then we went back to pick out the casket and vault. It is hard to pick out the casket, vault, and even the clothes for one of your children to be put in. There was conciliation; I knew my children belonged to the Lord. I knew Mike would have a better home, because we're promised a mansion if we know the Lord as our personal Savior, Praise the Lord. The casket had three crosses and said "In God's Care" on the inside lid. On the outside corners it had a cross and also one on the front. It was a pretty shade of blue.

After we finished selecting we went back into the office and made the rest of the arrangements and paid the bill.

He passed away on the 9th month, 9th day of 2009 at 2:04 p.m. on a Wednesday. We set the date for the funeral on Saturday the 12th of September at 1:00 p.m. at Bible Baptist Church. He was to be carried to the church, for viewing, one hour before the service.

After we left the funeral home, we went to the cemetery to meet the man there to show him where Mike was to be buried. We went to Wal-mart to pick out some clothes. I got underwear, socks, and picked out a blue striped shirt. I looked at some navy blue pants. I pondered and pondered. I went over to the overalls and I could just hear Mike, as he would pat the overalls and say, "Mom this is me." So I got the overalls. I knew Mike would have been pleased, because he loved overalls.

After we left Wal-mart we went to Smith's Florist to pick out his blanket. Sarah was a big help in picking out the flowers. They were assorted flowers that were light blue. They matched the casket and went with the blue striped shirt I had purchased. After I paid for the flowers we went back to Pecks to take the clothes. It seemed like we were in a whirlwind.

Finally, at last we had everything done and we went home. Frank and Sarah stayed awhile and they asked me if we would be okay. I knew it would be hard, but we would make it.

There was so much food brought in and it all had to be put away. Finally, at last everything was done and I went in and talked to Bonnie and gave her loving. She would look at me so seriously, like there are different things going on and she didn't understand exactly what.

When someone in the family passes away it seems you cannot get everything done. I think it's like going around in a circle. But, then you think about things that happened. Like, Hazel came out one day and was talking to Mike (this was when he could still talk a little). She asked him who she was; he looked at her and said, "Grandma". We had a good laugh because she does favor Mrs. Summerford a lot. Then, I think about the Patterson family we came to know thru Greg White, when he did bulldozer work and didn't charge anything. Isn't that just like the Lord? Their daughter, her boyfriend, and their two sons had a Bluegrass group. They came to sing for Mike and Bonnie a few times. They really enjoyed it.

I think about Carl, Hazel, and Kathy coming to see them. Hazel came many times when she wasn't able. I thought about the ones in my family that came to visit. I appreciated every visit that was made to see my children, because people seem to forget others when they get down.

Friday afternoon at 4:00 the hearse pulled up with Michael. It was the oddest thing; all at once Bonnie began to cry. You couldn't hear them when they pulled up. It was just like she knew. Bless her sweet heart, she loved her brother and he loved her.

Some of the pallbearers were there to help unload the casket and bring it into the house. Someone had asked me where I was going to put Mike. I said where his bed had been. I thought about some of my family members, also Jean and Sandra that helped. They cleaned my house up and we straightened my carport up. Mike and Sandra had taken Mike's bed to their house, so we would have room for the casket there.

I had told a few people, many years ago that if anything happened to the kids first, that I was going to bring them home. It was hard to leave my children at the funeral home. I knew that I was going to bring my babies home. That would be the last time that I would be able to spend with them, here upon this earth.

As people came to pay their respects, at least at the house we could have more time to spend together. I feel sure there were people that came to the house that probably wouldn't have gone to the funeral home.

Having Mike open at 4:00 p.m. gave people that couldn't see how to drive at night, time to visit and be home before dark. There were so many people that came. A lot of my family, people from church, friends, and friends I went to Austinville School with came. There were many tears shed, but there was also laughter. Mike was a kidder, he loved laughter. He would have enjoyed this visitation. It brings back to memory when Brother David and Trish Hicks were over children's church. That Christmas they all came Christmas caroling at our house. There were about fifty all total, and they went in and sang to Mike and Bonnie. After they were through, they all went and sat on the couch, floor or wherever while Brother David read them the Christmas Story.

It was such a blessing. Mike and Bonnie really enjoyed it. Churches don't go caroling like they used to. Let's get back to the ole time gospel way. Singing and even shouting as long as the Lord is in it.

After others had left, it was about 10:00 p.m., Carleen, Joe, Sandra, Meghan, Patsy, Freda, and I were all that was left. We pushed Bonnie in there to see Michael. At first she wouldn't look over at him. Then, at last she glanced over for a second. We took some pictures of her in there. I know that she realized he was dead, because that was her Bubba.

I was going to push her in to see him before they left with him going to the church. However, I changed my mind, I was afraid it would be too hard on her.

I know a lot of people wondered why I brought him home. You know we have gotten away from doing that. Like I have said before, I didn't want my babies left at the funeral home. Bonnie could see her Big Bubba one last time, also. Of course I know one day we will be reunited together again. Praise be to our Lord Jesus Christ for dying on the cross that made it possible (if we accept Christ) for us to have a way to go to Heaven. After the others left, Freda stayed awhile and we just visited. I needed that.

Well Saturday is here, the last day Mike will spend with us. David and Dustin came by early. Others began to come in. I thought to myself, Mike would have loved all the company. He enjoyed people coming by to visit. He loved the attention. The Lord is so good to us – I am thankful for all my wonderful family, friends, and brothers and sisters in Christ.

If it wasn't for the Lord I couldn't make it. Right in my heart and the pit of my stomach hurt with the loneliness I felt from missing Michael. No more beautiful smiles or no more loving here upon this earth. But, I know that he is whole again, walking and talking with the Lord. That is ground for shouting, "Praise the Lord."

Peck's Funeral Home came to pick Mike up at a little before 12:00, to take him to the church. He was to lie in state for one hour before the service. Jean stayed with Bonnie where Patsy and Meghan could go to the service.

We left the house about 12:40. As we arrived others of the family were in the front entry way. A lot of people had arrived and others continued coming in. As it neared 1:00 they began to usher us in. When we were seated, Steve, Ricky, and Johana began to sing. This is just a dream; it's time to wake up now I thought. Brother Jack opened with prayer. Brother Wendell told about Mike wanting a red Trans-Am and named the survivors. Brother Charles went to the 14th chapter of John (my favorite). You know a born again Christian can look forward to the place that the Lord had gone and prepared for us. That place is called Heaven.

As the people went around seeing Michael, it was as if my heart was breaking in two. My sweet darling, my first born was gone. But, thanks are to God I knew where he was. I couldn't help it but I was out of my seat before I knew it, and went up and kissed Mike on his forehead. That was where I always got my sweet loving from him.

As the service was over, we left the church to get into our vehicles. I rode with Frank and Sarah. The closer we got to Mount Tabor Cemetery the more my heart hurt. I knew it wasn't going to be long until Mike's body was going to be put in the ground.

When we got to the cemetery you could see the tent they had up and chairs under the tent. As we began to file out of our cars, Tim came over to me. It is a little steep going up to the graveyard. As we started up Tim got hold of my arm and held on to it. As we neared the chairs he stepped aside while I sat down. Then, he sat down beside me. Here we had a person whom is afflicted, but he knew what to do.

Shirley asked Wendell where Tim was and he pointed to where we were sitting.

Brother Charles said a few things and read some out of the Bible, and then he prayed. He and the undertakers shook hands with the family and gave words of condolences.

We went back to our cars and then we were to go to the church to eat. Some of the family didn't go. The food was delicious and there was plenty of it. When we finished, many of our relatives told the ladies of the church that the food was really good and thanked them for preparing it for us.

Frank and Sarah took me home when we finished eating, and they stayed awhile. After they went home, Jean stayed awhile and we talked. She said she needed to go home to prepare supper for Dick.

After everyone was gone, I went into Bonnie's bedroom to spend time with her. She could sense something was different. I told her how much that mother loved her and laid my head on her pillow and patted her.

When I prepared Bonnie's feeding I caught myself getting out Mike's things to feed him. I have done it for so many years; it just came natural for me to get his things out also.

Jean and I went back to the cemetery, late that afternoon, to take some pictures and to bring a few of the flowers home to dry.

As I got Bonnie ready for bed that night it didn't seem right not to have Mike there to get him ready. Although it's hard, life does go on.

Meghan came the next morning to stay with Bonnie for me to go to church. During the preaching service as the choir began to sing, I could feel the tears falling down my cheeks. I believe these are healing tears.

Days passed that I would go in to check on Bonnie and then start to check on Mike. He's not there anymore. He would get a big laugh out of that. I would get Bonnie's vitamins out and I'd look on the counter and I'd have Mike's out too.

As the days passed I could see a difference in Bonnie. I was still packing the abscess two to three times a day. She would have some good days, but I could see that her health all-in-all was going down.

Brother T. C. had offered to make some cabinets for my kitchen. At first I wasn't going to have him make the cabinets, but changed my mind. Brother Frank had offered a bunch of times, but I knew Mrs. Margaret was bad and he had plenty to do. Between Brother T. C. and Brother Frank they built cabinets that are in the kitchen, bookcases, corner cabinets, hung the bedroom door, built the front porch, and you name it. Thank you to my brothers in Christ.

Well it's Christmas. I want Bonnie to have a good Christmas. I put the tree up and decorated some for her. I put the cards around her doorway. I wanted it to be as normal a holiday as possible for her. The important thing to always remember is that Christmas was the birth of

Christ. Later on, He gave us the ultimate gift, which was His life. He died on the cross for each and every one of us. Just think the price He paid, because He loved us so much.

I got Bonnie a few things for Christmas, one was a new doll that gave a kiss. You can tell she don't like it. Shirley and I were talking before Christmas. We were talking about how Tim and Bonnie had everything. We didn't know what to get for them.

It sure is lonesome without Mike being here. I've said before, many times, he is in a better place. A lot better place than Bonnie and I are in. He's in the presence of the Lord. Can you imagine being right with the Lord, to look upon His face. This makes me want to shout "Praise the Sweet Lord."

The holidays have come and gone now. We try to get life back to normal, but of course it will never be the same.

Here it is January; Dr. Gandhi had called and said the antibiotic Bonnie was taking was not effective to the bacteria. It was going to take medication by IV'S's. He asked me how she was doing. I said right now she is doing fairly well. He said to call him when she wasn't feeling good. That was the 16th. By the 20th I had to call him. So here we are at the hospital. Blood was drawn and an x-ray of her chest was done.

When they were going to put the I.V. in she had no veins, so it took awhile for the nurse to get a needle in. She is taking Tobymycin twice a day and Zosyn three times a day. She has a yeast infection from taking the Cipro. They gave her Diflucan for three days.

Dr. Roberts came in to check on her bottom where the abscess is. He began to pack it with 2 feet of iodoform two times a day. Dr. Roberts is a very compassionate doctor with a lot of common sense. The nurses are so good to us. The kitchen always sends me a plate at mealtime and the food is delicious.

Bonnie's blood pressure began to go up and the nurse had to call Dr. Crouch (he was on call). He said to give her a mild blood pressure pill. Dr. Gandhi had to increase her thyroid medicine from 50 mcg. to 75 mcg. He wanted it checked again in six weeks. He told me if her blood pressure continued to be high that she would have to take blood pressure medicine. He wanted it checked twice a day. While talking with him I told him when she would get agitated her blood pressure would go up. He decided to put her on a mild nerve pill twice a day. On the 26th she got to go home. That was on a Tuesday. By Thursday night she was very agitated and her blood pressure was high.

The top half of her mouth to her throat was beet red and her tongue was broken out. It looked like it was parched. I gave her Tylenol to help with the pain. I called Susie on Friday morning. She called the hospital and talked to Dr. Vakaharia (he was on call). He called in one Diflucan. Jean stayed with Bonnie until I ran to pick it up. She whined off and on all day Saturday and Sunday, because her mouth hurt so much.

By Monday morning her mouth looked a little better but it wasn't well. I called Dr. Gandhi's office and talked with Ann, his nurse. I told her that her blood pressure was going up, but I thought it was because of her mouth. She called in for three Diflucan. That afternoon she called me back and told me Dr. Gandhi agreed with me. The pain from her mouth was causing her blood pressure to go up. You wouldn't think that having a yeast (or thrash) in the mouth would cause the blood pressure to go up. Believe you me (as the old saying goes) it sure does.

By Wednesday her mouth was nearly completely well and her blood pressure was down. Isn't that a blessing? Especially at night I get to thinking about Bonnie getting worse. Oh Lord, give me the strength and faith I need. I do know the Lord is not going to take her until He's ready for her. I think about Mike, oh how I miss him. This makes me cry. Half of my family is gone, half of my heart.

I had called Mrs. Phyllis and told her I wanted Brother Charles and the deacons to come over and anoint Bonnie with oil and pray over her. On Wednesday night (the 3rd of February) they came and anointed her and prayed for her. I know the Lord is going to touch her. Sometimes He uses doctors to do the healing and sometimes He does it Himself. I have seen many times in Michael, Bonnie, and my life that the Lord has stepped in to do the healing, and also to bring us out of the valley.

Bonnie began to have fever. I looked in her mouth and on each side of her tonsils was phlegm. I called the doctor on Monday morning and they called her in an antibiotic for her tonsils. I told him between the nerve pills she was getting agitated and her blood pressure was going up.

He said to give her one every eight hours. She is doing a lot better. She is more content. She doesn't whine like she did and her blood pressure is a good reading.

The wrong thing about nerve medicine is, if you need it and don't see a doctor for help. The other wrong thing is some people tend to get over medicated. Always follow the doctor's orders.

It's February now. Time passes so fast. Bonnie has been so sweet today. She smiled and even laughed out when I teased her about getting a valentine from her fellow. Meghan and I laughed so hard. It is such a blessing to see her so content. It is the first time, in a long time she has felt that good and been so content. Just one of God's blessings!

She is sleeping more lately, but she still sleeps well at night. I am so thankful for that. She is staring up at the ceiling again. She started that about two years ago. She will just look at the ceiling. I don't know if it is the shadow of the fan or she could be like Mike. Mike, I believe was looking for the Lord to come and get him.

Lord, I pray that my life would be a testimony to others. That people can see Christ in my everyday living and know that I live for Him to the best of my ability. Am I perfect, no – none of us are. But, we can go to I John 1:9 to ask the Lord to forgive us for our sins.

Bonnie was awake when I got up this morning. She was a little fussy, when I started to feed her. It caused her blood pressure to go up some.

Bonnie grinds her teeth, but I really have been in prayer that she would quit grinding them. She has really worn off the enamel. I have prayed that the Lord would not let the nerves be exposed. I know that all things are possible thru the Lord. Some people might say that it would be silly and useless for me to pray that. Some even look at you like you've lost your mind. But God's word says to "ask and you shall receive." I believe that all things are possible if it's the Lords will. For us to always give the Lord Jesus Christ the honor and glory for what He does.

I think Bonnie wakes up during the night and watches TV She has been awake the past seven days when I get up in the mornings. She then sleeps off and on during the day. I go in there and get me some smooches off her. She has a look on her face like an innocent baby. You know she is an innocent baby, in an adult body.

I thank my Heavenly Father for enabling me to be able to care for Bonnie and Mike, until the Lord called him home. Like I've said many times, they are my precious jewels.

She is looking up toward the ceiling again. Her blood pressure is up a little. I called Dr. Gandhi's office and talked to Ann. I explained about Bonnie having a problem. She said that she would call Home Health and get Susie to come out and do a culture.

We got the results and she does have a bacteria. Amoxicillin is the only medication sensitive to the bacteria, which she can take at home. If she is allergic to it, she will have to be put in the hospital with IV'S's. I have been in much prayer and asked others to pray that she won't be allergic to it.

Bonnie slept good last night. Praise God! So far she hasn't had any sign of a rash. Thank you Lord.

I didn't get to go to church last night. So I spent a lot of extra time with Bonnie. I teased her and she even laughed out, which that is such a blessing to me.

The sun is shining so beautiful today, although it's cold outside. The sunshine is another one of God's miracles. Have we ever thought about not being able to see the sunshine? There are a lot of people that can't see it because they are blind. There are a lot that can't talk or hear. I had a brother that couldn't talk or hear. Mother had German measles while she was pregnant with him and they settled in his ears and throat. We should be thankful for everything.

I was grateful for good health, but never gave it real concern. When Mike and Bonnie became ill, my way of thinking became serious. I was thankful to the good Lord for what good health that I had. It makes you think about a lot of things when you are confronted with different situations that you can't handle. We just have to turn everything over to the Lord and let Him handle the situations and not worry about them. It is hard for us, as humans, to give it to the Lord and leave it all with Him. So far, we've had a good day today. After lunch, when Jean came to sit with Bonnie, I went to the hospital to visit Barbara Wynn and Harold Ferguson. Barbara is in bad shape with the cancer she has. Harold needs prayer for salvation. But, he will let me pray with him, although sometimes he says yeah, I guess when I ask him if I can pray. Glenda said he's not as bad as he used to be about letting people pray for him. Lord, please take the scales off his eyes and the stone from around his heart, where he will get saved. It breaks my heart to think about someone dying and going to hell. Hell is forever, we know there is no turning back. I am so thankful that Mike knew the Lord Jesus Christ as his personal Savior. I know he has a mansion in Heaven, and he's walking and talking with the Lord. Praise the good Lord.

I woke up at 4:30 this morning and looked over and noticed Bonnie was already awake. Bless her little heart; she was laying there so sweet watching "Family Matters". I use to not be able to sleep with the TV or light on. Now, I'm use to it and I just sleep right on.

Well we got through another night with Bonnie taking her medication. Praise the Lord! She seems like she is feeling a lot better today. She has smiled a lot this morning. It is so sweet and a blessing to see her be content.

Patsy, Jennifer, and Tristen brought up the new baby tonight. We took him in for Bonnie to see. She was asleep when we first went into her room. I talked to her and finally got her awake, and then I laid the baby beside her. She just looked around while we took pictures. I wonder what she was thinking.

Another night has passed and she hasn't had any reaction yet. She does have 99.2° fever. She was whining when I got up this morning. It seems like every time Bonnie takes an antibiotic she runs a little fever. She was awake early again this morning. When she takes her 6:00 p.m. medication she will be halfway through with her antibiotic. Praise the Lord!

When I packed the abscess this morning, all you can see is a tiny speck that needs filling in. Then, it will just have to fill from the outside. Boy, I have shouting grounds. Praise the Lord! From today it has been one year, three months, and twenty-four days since it broke loose.

Bonnie was awake and whining this morning. I got up before 5:00 a.m. When I get to go to church, I really have to rush around to get things done. I give her thyroid medicine at 5:00 a.m., feeding at 6:00. In between those times I brush her teeth, take her blood pressure and temperature, make my bed and wash up the dishes. I glance at the deaths in the newspaper. I read my Bible and eat my breakfast. At 7:00 I turn Bonnie onto her side. That is a typical two hours of my morning every day. Do I get tired, sure I do, but I wouldn't have it any other way.

Bonnie began to whine when I got up. She acts like she doesn't feel good. I took her temperature and it was 100.2°. I called Dr. Gandhi's office and left a voice message for Ann. She called me right back and said she would call Levaquin and Bactrim in for Bonnie. She was to take the rest of the other medication first. She finished it on Wednesday at 12:00. Then, Thursday she starts the other two medications. I pray that these will make her feel a lot better. I talk to Ann about Bonnie's infection still being there. She told me she would have Susie to get another culture, to not start on the other medication until we found out the results. I pray that she doesn't have to go into the hospital. She doesn't do well at the hospital and her mother doesn't either. The nurses and staff are always so good to us but Bonnie likes being at home and her schedule changes also. Although we do try to keep her on a schedule, as much as possible, while she is in the hospital.

It sure has rained this morning. The Lord knows that we are going to need that moisture in the ground this summer when it gets so dry. We should be thankful for every raindrop that falls our way. Doesn't the Bible say to be thankful for everything?

It was stormy last night and early this morning. I sure was glad that the power didn't go off. If it goes off, I have to put Bonnie on the other bed and sometimes it is hard to do.

I'm going to see Barbara after lunch. She sure is low. She has been a fighter. Praise the Lord she's ready to cross over soon.

As I was getting ready I went in to talk to Bonnie for a few minutes. I talked to her about Michael. I told her when I would talk to Mike I'd say, "Mike who do I love" and he would say, "Me." She grinned so sweet. I would say, "What is your sissy's name?" He would say, "Bonnie." This was before he quit talking. It sure blesses my heart to see her smile.

When Dick brought my mail over this morning I could see another long, business type envelope. I thought boy it sure is awful thick. I opened it up and it had $40 in it with a note. It sure does come in handy. It is another blessing from the Lord.

Bonnie has been fretful today. But at least she has been able to sleep off and on the biggest part of the day. I know she is waking up sometime during the night, because she has been awake every morning for awhile when I get up. She will lay there quietly until about the time for me to get up. Maybe she wants me to stay in bed and not make any racket, where she can watch TV in peace and quiet.

Well, talk about being a night owl. Bonnie's bed went off at 3:30 this morning. I didn't get to go to bed until late on account of giving Bonnie her medication. When I got up this morning, she was wide awake watching television.

Brother Charles preached a good message from the book of Romans this morning. Brother Andy preached tonight from II Corinthians, his message was good too. He told us that he had accepted the position as pastor at a church in upper New York. They had gone up there and stayed about two weeks for him to preach trial sermons. Brother Andy will make a great pastor. We will be in much prayer for them, Brother Charles, and Mrs. Phyllis. I know it will be a big change for Brother Charles and Mrs. Phyllis, with them being use to having those babies around.

God opens doors and you know that it is the hand of God that works things out in peoples' lives. Things fall into place because we know that it is God that has the pathway for us to follow. I pray for God to lead, guide, and direct my life. I went to see Barbara again today, she sure is bad. God will be ushering her into Heaven soon. She said she is ready to go to meet her dear Lord.

Bonnie is so sweet, she's mothers darling angel. I would sing gospel songs to Mike and Bonnie. I'd just make them up and sing to them. They would just smile so sweetly. It would melt your heart. That's another good memory of Mike.

Well Bonnie stayed awake about all afternoon. She is just laying there so content and watching television. But, she slept some this morning while I was gone to the ladies Tuesday morning prayer meeting. Dr. Gandhi's office called at 3:00 this afternoon. Ann told me they called in an antibiotic called Doxycycline. She said the cultures came back that Bonnie had a staph infection. I asked her what precaution I should take and she told me the doctor said just to make sure I keep my hands washed. So I knew it wasn't the really bad kind. She will take two of the capsules a day for seven days. I pray that this will get rid of the staph infection. So far Bonnie has not had any reaction to the antibiotic. I started her on it last night at 5:30. She stayed awake a good portion of the day. I know there are times she gets her days and nights mixed up. To her it doesn't matter. I am so thankful that she is content a lot of the time now.

Patsy came up to sit with Bonnie so I got to go to church. Joann came and went with me. Brother Charles taught on Proverbs. It was a good lesson. I count it a privilege to get to go to church each week, to all three services. It is such a blessing because we really don't know what tomorrow might bring.

Bonnie slept some this morning. When we got ready to give her bath she began to whine. She started to have blotches on her chest and upper arms. With her taking an antibiotic you would think she was having an allergic reaction to it, but it's not. When she gets upset she will do that, so it's just her nerves. After she gets over being upset it will all go away.

Doris called me this morning to tell me about Barbara Wynn passing away. She has had a long hard struggle. She had battled this for over four years. Praise the Lord she's well now.

It is so nice and pretty today. It was a little cool this morning, but it warmed up a lot this afternoon. It's supposed to be in the 70's tomorrow. Maybe I can get a lot done outside, when Meghan gets here tomorrow.

I worked off and on a good portion of the day. It has been a beautiful day. When I came in at 2:00 I told Meghan that I could tell I was getting older. I was plum tired. At 2:30 I went back to give Bonnie her medicine. I started talking to her and she started to whine a tad. I said everything was okay that I had been here all day and I hadn't gone anywhere. She began to laugh a little. She was so sweet; I just wanted to squeeze her good. She acts like she feels real good. I am so thankful dear Lord.

We have had a good weekend. Bonnie has done so well. When I got in from church tonight, I told Patsy that I felt like something bad was going to happen. I just had this awful feeling. I couldn't shake it and my heart felt so burdened. I cried out to the Lord. Lord, I know that our church needs prayer too. I need to get back to the down on my knees in prayer time. Lord help us!

Well, they said it was going to rain, turning into snow today. Guess what, that's what happened. We got snow.

I was brushing Bonnie's teeth this morning when a piece of the tooth that Dr. Hawkins made around the pins came out. At first, I saw the piece that was broken and couldn't figure out where it came from. I looked at Bonnie's teeth and couldn't find a missing piece. Bonnie then reared her head back and started to whine and as she did I could see the missing piece. It was next to her front tooth.

Right then and there I started praying for Bonnie about going to the dentist. I didn't worry, I was just in prayer. To a lot of people this in not a big ordeal; but in this household it sure is. I called and made an appointment for tomorrow. I wasn't sure if it could be fixed or if it would have to be pulled. I called Doris to tell her I wouldn't be able to come to the ladies prayer meeting and why. I wanted them to remember Bonnie in prayer. You see, I believe in prayer. I got a phone call from Nancy, my sister-in-law, this morning. She said they put Richard, my brother, in ICU, he wasn't doing well. I told her I had to take Bonnie to the dentist but I will be down there afterwards.

Bonnie's appointment is at 1:00 so the ambulance came at 12:30. When we got there they put Bonnie into one of Tina's rooms. As she came in I told her that Bonnie hadn't been well enough for me to bring her to have her teeth cleaned. She said that while Bonnie was there she would polish her teeth. When she was through, she said there would be no charge. Isn't that a blessing? Tina had taken four x-rays. When Dr. Greg and Glenda came in, he looked at the x-rays and said the tooth was still in place. He filled the back side of it. Glenda said I could tell the ambulance drivers that we were ready. When I got back I asked for the bill and Glenda said there was no charge. Isn't that just like the Lord? We have a lot to be thankful for.

Bonnie was so tired, that Patsy said she slept the whole time I was gone to see my brother.

Richard sure did look bad, he didn't even know me. He looked at me like he was trying to figure out who I was. I stayed also for the 8:00 visiting hour. Carleen, my niece and I went to chick-Fila and ate. I got to spend some time with her. She wouldn't have it any other way than to pay for our supper. Wasn't that so sweet? I'm not use to eating out much. I guess I'm the stay at home type. I love being at home with Bonnie.

I do miss not being able to do some things at church. I miss not being able to go to all the revivals we have. But, we don't know what tomorrow might bring so I enjoy and savor every moment I get to spend with Bonnie.

I went to see Richard on Wednesday, and he wasn't doing any better.

Bonnie and I spent all day on Thursday together. The nurse came to change her catheter, G-tube, and to draw blood. The bath girl came at 11:30, so after lunch Bonnie and I just spent time together. She likes for me to talk to her. She will just look at me while I'm talking. I wonder many times what she's thinking.

I received a book in memory of Michael. There were seven businesses around town that sponsored the book. It was so nice.

When I went to see Richard today, he was a lot better. He looked at me and I asked him if he knew who I was. He said, "Yes, you're Edith." I knew then he was a lot better, for now. For how long, God only knows. Just like the song "One Day at a Time" that is what we all need to do. Just take each day and live for the Lord because we don't know what tomorrow might bring.

Bonnie seems to be better right now. She is more content and doesn't whine as much as she did. It is sure a blessing to see her like this. She has certain TV programs she likes and she is really enjoying them.

We had a good service at church today. Brother Charles preached a good message. I pray the people that have gotten out of church would come back. Like I've said, our church family is our family. When they aren't there, we miss them.

We had a fellowship supper for Brother Andy and Rachel after the Sunday night service. They will be leaving a week from tomorrow. We hate to see them go. We pray there will be many souls for his labor. I know Brother Charles and Mrs. Phyllis hate to see them go, but they will do just fine.

God is so good to us. We have plenty to eat, a good house to live in, a car to drive, and bills are paid. Of course I miss Mike so much, there's no comparison to missing him. Brother Wyman said last night that he'd heard I had lost one of mine. Yes, but I know he's in a better place I told him. A lot of people can't say that about their son or daughter. Thanks are to our Lord that Mike and Bonnie both accepted the Lord and were baptized. That is something we can't do for our children. It is left up to each individual which road to take - the broad road to hell or the straight and narrow road to heaven.

It is so beautiful today. The cherry bushes, plum and peach trees are in full bloom. You can see the hand of the Lord in all these things. Praise God, Praise God, Praise God, give thanks and glory to God almighty.

Here it is the 30th day of March. Bonnie is mighty quiet – really too quiet. She sure has watched me today. She just stares at me, not taking her eyes off me to watch TV; though she acts contended, but real tired. I can look at her eyes and tell that she is weak. God bless her little heart she has been through a lot. Mike had been through a lot too before he passed away. The Lord had His hand upon them and He still does Bonnie. I have really been blessed.

I wish I had started writing many years ago, but it might not have been meant to be. If I had, there would be so much more that I could remember. You know the saying "I'm not as young as I use to be" is true. As we get older we forget things.

Bonnie sure has been quiet, but contented these last few days. She is just laying there watching TV. Just knowing that she's watching TV is a blessing.

I invited Brother Andy, Rachel, Mr. Reese, and the babies over for supper tonight. We had good fellowship and seemed like they enjoyed their meal. I know Brother Andy and his family is going to be a great asset to the church and the community they are moving to.

We had a good Easter service today. The church wasn't nearly full, but we had quite a few visitors. I pray the church would be overflowing with people. There wasn't but four of us besides Doris in our Sunday school class. It's a shame there wasn't more. I pray that God would deal with each and every member that doesn't attend. He would burden their heart till they came back to church and each one would be on fire for Him.

I didn't get to go to the Sunday night service. Patsy and her family had a cookout at her sisters and she couldn't stay with Bonnie. I told her that it was fine. I'd spend time with my precious Bonnie. I've been in here writing and talking with Bonnie while she watches me. When I gave her the Easter card this morning and read it to her she cried. She has such a tender heart.

I knew Brother Charles and Mrs. Phyllis were really down. So, I invited them over to eat. Thursday night they came and we sup together, as the saying goes. We had some good fellowship together. I enjoyed having them at my house. There's nothing like having fellowship with God's people. We went in to see Bonnie and she was trying to smile at them. It's between a mixed laugh and cry. She is such a dear.

I went to see Richard and spent a good portion of the day with him. Gladys, Karen, and Madeline were there. He looks a lot better than he did Wednesday, but he still looks bad. He's supposed to go home Monday afternoon. Dr. Putnam said to take him home and make him comfortable. He's been on a long journey of pain with his legs for years. God bless his heart he has been a strong man to be as old as he is. He will be 84 on September 11th.

Bonnie sure has been smiling a lot lately. It will bless your heart to see her smile. When I talk to her she will open her little mouth and smile at me. I can just picture Mike when he would open his mouth so big. Then, he would have that big smile on his face. My heart aches and I have times that I cry for a spell. I do know he is in a better place, but that doesn't take the hurt of missing him away. It just isn't the same. When Mike was born and then Bonnie, it was always the three of us. I am so thankful the good Lord gave me 48 years with Mike. A lot of people didn't think they would live as long as he did and as long as Bonnie has.

I got a call yesterday from Ann about Bonnie's culture from around her catheter. She said there was a bacteria around it. The doctor called in Bactrim D S. Bonnie is to take it twice a day for seven days. Here's another prayer to be prayed, that she can take the antibiotic without any reaction. I started her antibiotic when I gave her 6:00 p.m. feeding. That way I can keep an eye on her. I always have Benadryl next to her if I need it. So far, I haven't had to use any. Praise the Lord.

When I went in this morning to check Bonnie's blood pressure and to turn her, I noticed she was breathing a little on the hard side. She was asleep, but was breathing deep. So far she is doing fine with the antibiotic.

I'm going to stay a while with Richard and Gladys. Then, go see Madeline and Bill to see the house they bought.

Richard said he wasn't feeling good. He is real weak and I know he's tired of laying there. I spent a while with them and left to go see Madeline and Bill. I pray that her and Bill would get in church. It would be such a blessing to me. I stayed a while then left. They sure have a nice place.

When I got home Bonnie was so quiet and content. I went in to talk to her and get me a bunch of loving. She is so sweet. She looks at me when I talk to her. She looks like a little angel. Well today is Saturday and Bonnie really is fretful this morning. I believe it is her antibiotic that is making her feel like this. When I looked at her catheter bag I noticed the urine was dark and there wasn't much in it. The urine was also thick. She has been on the antibiotic for two and one half days, so maybe it is working to get all of the impurities out of her kidneys. She will feel better then.

She has whined just about all day long. She would get irritated because she tried to go to sleep, but would wake right up after only a few minutes. Finally, at last she went to sleep at bedtime.

She slept fairly good last night. I sure was proud. I know it wears her out when she doesn't sleep well. Bless her little heart she can't tell me how she feels – if she hurts anywhere, I just have to guess.

I know people may wonder why I'm keeping a day by day journal now. I want others to know even if times get hard or we're way down deep in that valley, the Lord is always there with His outstretched hands to help us. He loved us with an everlasting love. God sent His son to die on the cross for us. John 3:16 says, "For God so loved the world that he gave his only begotten Son, that whosoever believeth in him should not perish but have everlasting life" (King James Version 1611, John 3:16). There are things that I want to remember. In the past I didn't write everything down and I had to go by memory.

Bonnie finished her antibiotic this morning, but she still has a thickness to her urine. She has been more content today, but is looking at the ceiling more. She doesn't watch TV like she used to. She will watch me when I am in her room. Mike did the very same thing. I know the Lord is not going to take her until He is ready. He knows when the time is right.

I got to go to revival tonight. Brother Billy Gosby held a three day revival for us. Brother T. D. Burgess was supposed to hold it. The Lord knew who to send and what we needed. It sure was a blessing. I wished I could have gone the other two nights, but it wasn't possible. We need revival. I need revival.

It sure did rain hard, but we really needed the rain. It was so dry that the ground had begun to crack.

I didn't get to go to church today, maybe Patsy will come and I can go tonight. Meghan is not with us anymore. She sure was a good worker and we sure did love her. A new girl came today, but I won't leave Bonnie with a new person. I stay around them awhile and Bonnie gets used to them.

Patsy came up tonight to sit with Bonnie, so I did get to go to church. I looked around when I went in and it broke my heart to see so many empty pews. The brothers and sisters in Christ should have been in the house of God. We need the Lord. The things that are happening and the way the economy is, makes me realize more than ever that the Lord wants us more on our knees in prayer. The Bible says to pray without ceasing. The way I read that, it means to always have a prayer in our mind, heart, and on our lips.

Karen called me this morning and told me that her daddy was in ICCU again. She said her mother had to call 911 about 9:30 last night. I had talked to Gladys about 6:00 last night. Karen said it was congestive heart failure. I went down this afternoon to see him, he looked worse than before. I talked to my brother, Fletcher after the 6:00 p.m. visitation and he said he was bad off. I would like to have gone back for the 8:00 visitation, but I don't like going to the parking lot at Decatur General after dark. Gladys has taken such good care of Richard for a lot of years. Some wives would have put their husband in a nursing home. Gladys has really stuck by Richard.

Well I went down today to see Richard. I can see he is really bad. His breathing is labored. I got back home about 3:30. I got a call at 6:10 from Dorothy Jean. She told me to call the rest of the family. The doctor said we had better come if we wanted to see him alive. Patsy came up to sit with Bonnie and I called the rest of the family. Then, I took off for the hospital. I was too late, he had already passed away. We stayed around and then went back to see him.

Visitation was on Sunday night from 6 to 8. I saw a lot of my relatives that I hadn't seen in a long time. It is so sad that it takes a death in the family to get people together.

I was so thankful that we had the family reunion. It was after Michael had passed away. I wish we could have had it when he was still alive, but he wasn't up to it. Richard had been real sick too. He really enjoyed himself though and said so. It seems like everybody enjoyed themselves. It was so good to see him smiling, we'll have that memory.

Richard was buried on Monday at Mt. Tabor. That makes two girls and two boys, of my siblings, who have already gone on. It leaves two girls and two boys. He sure will be missed. I love my siblings. We were raised up during hard times and were taught to be hard workers. I pray for Gladys, Karen, and Wes. It will be so hard on them.

Bonnie slept off and on all day yesterday and today. I am so glad that she is able to rest. So far, she is still able to sleep good at night. Thank you Lord for her being able to sleep!

May 20, 2010, Bonnie sure has been a lot quieter for the last few days. It seems like she is getting weaker. Lord, you know our future. Help me Lord, give me the strength and faith that I need. She's my precious little darling. I call her my Little Tater Bug. I see beyond her whining. I see the love that she has always had for the Lord, the testimonies that she has given, and for never failing to ask prayer for her daddy. She did this although it was hard for her to talk, she couldn't get all the words out, without having a hesitation in her speech. Mike and Bonnie were always good kids, even when they were small.

Yesterday morning and this morning Bonnie had started whining real early. Her blood pressure has been up since the 17th of this month. May 24th her blood pressure was 155/115. First thing when I got up, I checked it. She's not feeling well. I called Dr. Gandhi's office and talked to Ann. She said for me to check it every so often, chart it, and call her back in the morning.

I called her this morning and gave her the blood pressure readings. Dr. Gandhi called me after lunch and said he was leaving it up to me to decide if Bonnie wasn't feeling that good. I felt like she really needed to be put in the hospital. I told him that Susie was coming to change her feeding tube and catheter and I would see what she thought. When she looked at Bonnie she said yes, that she needed to go to the hospital.

So here we are. It is 9:00 p.m. and she has already taken a bag of gentamicin and a bag of Fortaz in her IV. I pray she can take the medication without any allergic reaction.

When Dr. Gandhi came by to check on Bonnie, he said her immune system was low. He asked me when she started getting worse. I said the 17th of this month. Her blood pressure started to go up and she has been having a low grade fever. You can look at her and tell she doesn't feel good at all.

All the doctors and nurses have always been so nice to us. They were so good to Mike when he was alive and always to Bonnie, too. I thank God for that.

Bonnie made it through the night. The medicine has not made her break out so far. She even seems like she feels a little bit better. She is paying more attention to the television. I thank God for the knowledge that He has given the doctors and the labs that make all the medications. Without them it would take a touch from our Lord and Savior. Each one of us must realize where everything comes from. Without our Lord Jesus Christ we are nothing. Do you know Him as you personal Savior? If you don't know Him, today is the day that you need to let Him come into your life. If you ask the Lord to forgive you for your sins, and mean it from the bottom of your heart, He is just and will forgive you and cover your sins with His blood. Never to be remembered anymore. He is God's son and He arose the 3rd day. Makes me want to shout, "Thank you Lord for dying on the cross for us, you made a way for an old sinner like me." We go to Him "Just as I am." Even we as Christians have. I John 1:9 confess our sins (we do sin daily). He is faithful and just to forgive us our sins and to cleanse us from all unrighteousness. Lord, why didn't I accept you as my Savior years and years ago. Oh, the strength that you have given me. If I hadn't had you in my life when Mike passed away, I couldn't have made it. You are my strength, my fortress.

Dr. Gandhi came in this morning and said he was starting Bonnie on a blood pressure pill. He was going to New York so Dr. Vora was going to be on call for him. He started talking to Bonnie trying to get her to smile at him. She smiled the biggest, sweetest smile for him and it tickled him. At last she did give him a smile.

Bonnie started on her blood pressure pill at 1:00 today. So far she is doing okay. They haven't checked her blood pressure yet, she has been awake the biggest part of the day. Maybe she will sleep well tonight. Doris and Mrs. Phyllis came by for a visit. We sure were glad to see them. It sure gets boring while you're in the hospital, as a patient or either a caregiver. There isn't enough to do.

I talked to Sandra earlier and she told me they put JoAnn at Summerford's for 21 days. It sure was good to hear from her. She gave me JoAnn's number, so I called to talk to her a few minutes. I didn't talk long because I knew she didn't feel good. She said therapy was awful. Bless her heart, we love her.

At 4:15 p.m. the R.N. checked Bonnie's blood pressure, and it was 123/74. It has come down a good bit. I pray this little 2.5 mg pill will do the job. Her blood pressure was up at 9:00 p.m. It was 160/101, but she was really agitated. I knew it was going to be up. Lord, help it to level off and be like it's supposed to be. I pray that we have a good night's rest tonight.

She slept pretty good last night but her fever was up to 100.3° this morning. I figure she has a kidney infection. Dr. Vora came in this morning. He requested an x-ray to be taken of her chest. He said she had a U.T.I. infection. They are doing the culture and sensitivity to see what grows out. However, it will probably be tomorrow before we hear from it. I pray the antibiotics, she is on, is sensitive to the bacteria she has. If not we will have to start all over again. That will make her have to stay longer in the hospital.

The nurse checked Bonnie's blood pressure about 12:00 and it was 120/84. That was a good reading. Thank you Lord Jesus.

We have had a lousy day. Dr. Vora said Bonnie's chest x-ray showed a little of her lung was collapsed, but it was not unusual for someone in her condition. The reason is she can't breathe deep. Her culture and sensitivity test came back okay. Praise the good Lord. He said the IV'S's she was getting would take care of the U.T.I. infection. Maybe she can go home earlier. It would be nice to be in our own beds tonight.

Patsy and Junior came this morning. It was good to see them. They've lived behind us for 13 years and they seem just like family. Brother Steve and Joyce came by and we had such good fellowship. We've known them for 27 years and they have been a blessing to us. It wasn't long after they left that Neysa, from church, came by and stayed awhile. It sure was a blessing to see her. When visitors come by it sure makes the time pass by a lot faster. There were a few phone calls which helped a lot.

Bonnie has slept just about all afternoon. I know it is because she had fever and we gave her some liquid Tylenol. Her fever was 100.6°. I pray the medication will take care of everything and her fever will go down. Like I said before, when Bonnie is on antibiotics she will run a fever. She slept all afternoon, and she slept good last night.

After I had bathed her this morning, the nurse came in to check her blood pressure. It was real high so she waited a while before she checked it again. When she checked it this time it was still high, but it had come down some. She just doesn't want anybody to bother her. Bless her heart she just wants to lay there, watch TV, and be content. I can't say that I blame her.

She sure has problems this afternoon. Around her catheter is leaking. It gets her 4x4, gown, and top sheet wet. I'm sure she is having bladder spasms. I've changed her four times within a five hour period. It breaks my heart to see her hurt and can't do anything about it. I can pray that the Lord will help her, that she will feel better.

Bonnie feels better this morning with her spasms. She sure seems weaker though and breathing down deep from the bottom of her stomach. Her oxygen level checked out good. It was 98.

When Dr. Vora came by this morning, I told him about Bonnie having problems yesterday afternoon. He ordered another chest x-ray, upper stomach and one on the lower stomach, and another urine specimen.

She has been doing better this afternoon. More content and she even watched TV. She even let me get a bunch of loving from her, and didn't whine a bit. It is such a blessing to see her like this, to not be in pain like she was yesterday.

It is 5:30 p.m. and I've been talking to Bonnie, telling her how much I love her. You would not believe the most beautiful smile that she gave me. That is the most that I have seen her smile in a long time. Right now she seems so happy. I am so thankful for that. It feels my heart with joy to see her smile. Bonnie used to smile like that all the time; I sure have missed all those beautiful smiles.

Bonnie slept well, all night last night. We're waiting on Dr. Vora to come by. I pray that he says she can go home today. She will be more satisfied at home. She knows this is not her room. She may not be able to talk or to comprehend a lot of things, but she knows when there is a change.

I know some people wonder why she whines. Just think if you couldn't talk what would you do? Me, I'd probably whine too. You see, that is her way of communication.

Dr. Vora came by and said the x-ray of her intestines showed she had something there. The x-ray technician thought it was an abscess. Dr. Vora thinks that it is feces there. He ordered a bottle of Magnesium Citrate to be given to her. Then, he wanted another stomach x-ray done tonight. He said she would probably get to go home tomorrow. I would love to take Bonnie home today, but I want to make sure everything is okay. I don't know how long it will take for the Nitrate to work. Bonnie's intestines are slow working, bless her heart she can't help it.

Here it is 7:00 and the Citrate hasn't worked yet. I will turn her back over at 9:00 to see if she has had any results or not. Some people might think its gross, but it's a natural thing.

She didn't have any results last night, but I turned her on her side about 6:45 this morning. I got some results back, but I don't know if she got cleaned out enough or not. They will take another x-ray of her stomach. I told the technician that she did the best that she could.

Dr. Vora came in this morning with a smile, saying that it was all gone. Thank you dear Lord, another prayer answered.

Bonnie was dismissed, so I can take her home. After we got home, she slept the rest of the evening. She was so worn out. It really takes a toll on her to be moved around, and the ride from the hospital just wears her out.

Bonnie's stay in the hospital was made so much easier with the good care that she received at Hartselle Medical Center. The doctors and nurses are dedicated, and they have compassion for their patients.

Bonnie's infection is gone, but she looks so weak in her eyes. Dr. Gandhi told me her immune system was getting weaker. I really, down deep, already knew that. I am with her so much that I can see her getting a little weaker each day. I've said many times, "The Lord's not going to take her until He's ready." We don't know He may come back after His children before then. Praise the Lord, come quickly. I think about some of my loved ones and friends that are lost. It saddens me so much, but they have that choice to accept Christ or not. I would do it for them if I could, but it doesn't work that way.

Bonnie still looks weak and hasn't felt good. Today is the 12th of June. She has whined the biggest part of the day. I know something is wrong. She has whined so much, she has whined herself to sleep.

I called Dr. Gandhi's office and Ann called back and said Dr. Gandhi wanted me to take her to the emergency room.

When we got to the emergency room Dr. Richardson was the emergency room doctor. They took blood work, oxygen level, urine specimen, and a chest x-ray. I knew her tonsils and throat were red. When the doctor came in, he said all her test came back okay, but she had an upper respiratory infection. He gave her a prescription and we went home.

She took it once a day for seven days. I could tell after a few days she was feeling better. Then, by Wednesday of the next week she started about 2:00 that afternoon and whined until she went to sleep that night. On Thursday Dr. Gandhi called in her a prescription of clarithromycin to be given every six hours around the clock. Thank you Lord for the medications that you have allowed the scientists to discover to help people.

Well Bonnie has two more days of medication left. Thursday at noon will be her last dose. No allergic reaction, but she has gotten a yeast infection in her mouth. Dr. Gandhi called in for three days of Diflucan. Boy, you can tell a difference when the medicine starts to work.

I went into Bonnie's room and started talking to her and she gave me one of her beautiful smiles. It was such a blessing to see her smile again.

Mike's birthday was the 30th of June. I went on the 29th and put flowers on his grave. I couldn't go on the 30th; it was easier to go the day before. I know he's not here, but that's the last place I saw him before he was put in the ground.

Well a few days after she had taken all of the medication she began to whine again, even in her sleep. I don't know what is wrong except her allergies are acting up. That could be it, but she's taking her Zertec.

She may be aggravated because it's draining into her throat. There is a possibility that it is the muscular dystrophy is getting worse. Her eyes look so peeked.

Saturday, the 10th of July, wow its Bonnie's birthday. I sang "Happy Birthday" to Bonnie and gave her presents. I took pictures of her. Years ago I didn't get to take pictures of Michael and Bonnie because I couldn't afford it. I said when I could afford to I would take pictures, because that is good memories to look at. Shirley sent Bonnie a check for her birthday and Madeline sent her money. I got her a doll that kissed and said, "I love you," maybe I got it for myself (I remember getting only one doll when I was little). I also got her a pretty gown. I told Bonnie that with the money from Shirley and Madeline I could get her a couple more gowns. She loves pretty things with bright colors.

For the last week Bonnie has not slept well. She wakes up between 2:30 to 4:00 whining a little. This morning she slept until 4:50, which was a lot better. I don't know if it's her allergies, muscular dystrophy, or if there is a possibility she has a kidney infection. She has been running fever from 99.2° to 99.9°. Every morning she has fever. Bless her heart, sometimes you just have to guess what's wrong.

On Wednesday the 28th, at about 4:00 a.m., I had to jump up and help Bonnie. She was breathing hard and her heart rate was very rapid. I rolled the head of her bed up real high and I began to pray. She was breathing like Mike did before he passed away, just not as hard. I began to rub her arm and talk to her. The Lord came through. She began to breathe better and her heart rate slowed down and beat like it was supposed to. Thank you dear Lord! It wasn't long until she went back to sleep. I just stayed up because I knew I was going to have to call the doctor's office when they opened. I called at 8:00 and told about her fever, blood pressure elevation, her difficulty breathing and her rapid heart rate. It wasn't long until Ann called and said they were sending Home Health out. They were to take blood and a urine specimen. Karen came after lunch. She did blood work and got a urine specimen.

On Thursday afternoon, about 2:30, Dr. Gandhi called and told me that Bonnie's white blood cell count was 15,000 and that it was suppose to be 10,000. So he put her on Amoxicillin two times a day for seven days. He said if that didn't take care of it, he would put her in the hospital.

She seems to be tolerating the medicine good so far. Thank the good Lord again. If it wasn't for the Lord, I don't know what we would do. We sure would be in a lot of trouble trying to work things out on our own.

Well, I started to Sunday school a little early this morning. I thought Doris sure will be surprised because it's generally 9:55 a.m. when I get here. As I got nearly to the highway I noticed Janice and Mike (her son-in-law) were stopped at the end of the road. Janice had her water meter lid up. I thought are they having water problems? As I got up where they were Mike came over and said, "Mrs. Summerford, you have major water problems." I looked and water was all in the ditch and I was even watering Brother Nathan Green's pasture. I know the horses were proud of that.

As I looked at my meter, it was covered with water. I could see a gushing of water shooting up out of the meter. I thanked them and began to back up to the house to call the water department. Jean came out to see what was wrong. I told her about the water – I couldn't say leaking out, but gushing out. I told Patsy to draw up some water because we didn't know how long the water would be off or what was wrong. Then, I called the water department. I drew up water for the kitchen and bathroom too. I didn't want to run out. The young man was here in less than 10 minutes, boy I sure was thankful. I had been gracious enough for one day with my water. As he turned the water off, I heard the dreaded words, "I'm sorry, but it is on your side of the meter." I told him, but I've been praying that it would be on your side. Maybe I was being selfish, but I can just see that water bill.

There goes my being at Sunday school on time. At least I made it by 10:30, so I was able to hear some of it. Doris is teaching on leading people to the Lord and what scripture to use.

I called Keith about my problem. He came this afternoon to see what was wrong. He dug down to the reducer and found the problem. He said it would be in the morning before he could fix it because he would have to get the parts.

He was here bright and early this morning. He got it fixed except a tiny drip. He said he would be back this afternoon with a larger vise grip to tighten it, so it wouldn't drip. Sure enough, this afternoon he was back to finish the job like he said he would. I sure was thankful I could even breathe a lot easier knowing that it was fixed.

I had to call the doctor about Bonnie's mouth because it is broken out and real red. They called her in 150 mg. of Diflucan for three days. So, I started her on it this Monday afternoon.

Tuesday afternoon I walked around to the back side of the house. I noticed that it was damp about two feet on each side of my dryer vent. I thought, "Oh no, what is wrong this time?" I knew we hadn't had any rain. I went into the house to the utility room and looked. The sheet rock was wet behind the dryer. I felt of the wall and it was hot, so I knew it was the hot water line. Here goes filling up more pots and jugs so we can have plenty of water. I went outside and cut the water off.

"Hey Tater (Keith)," I said. He answered, "Yes." "I've got a water leak in the utility room behind the dryer," I told him. He said it would be Wednesday afternoon before he could get to it. He was installing a central unit the next morning.

True to his word, he was there Wednesday afternoon. He cut a piece of the sheet rock out and found the problem. He went to get parts, and it didn't take long for him to fix it. I'm sure glad God gives each person different talents, because mine sure isn't plumbing.

I called Shirley to tell her "Tater" had my problem fixed. I had w-a-t-e-r. We don't realize how precious water is until we don't have it. We use to have to draw water from a well. But, we got modernized and just turn the little ole facet on. I sure am glad that we did go modern on that. Thank you dear Lord!

Bonnie took her last dose of medicine this morning, which is Thursday. She has been sleeping more and more. She goes through stages of sleeping good and then staying awake at night. It reminds me of a baby getting their days and nights mixed up.

Here it is Friday and Bonnie's mouth is worse than what it was. I called the Morgan County Home Health and told the nurse. She called the hospital, and Dr. Gandhi called in 6 of 100 mg Diflucan. She was to take one a day for six days. I called NPHC about Bonnie's G-tube. It was growing something black inside of her tube. I asked if maybe it could be mold. She didn't know.

Although Bonnie's mouth hurts she has been so sweet. She even tries to smile. She reminds me of Mike with his sweet smile. Oh it still hurts so badly losing Mike. I get his picture, with that big ole smile, so I have to have my crying spell and then it is better for awhile. I know where he is and I'll see him again one day. He's probably saying, "Mom why are you crying?"

NPHC said that Home Health's nurse could come and take a culture of the black stuff in Bonnie's tube. I told her the nurse was supposed to come Monday to do blood work (to see if her white blood count had gone down). They wanted her G-tube changed. It had been changed three weeks ago. It's supposed to be changed every two months.

She slept about all afternoon Sunday. Then she slept real well Sunday night. I was so proud. I was afraid as much as she had slept, she would be awake half the night. Thank you Lord!

The nurse came today and changed the G-tube. She cut it open and swabbed around for a culture. She stuck Bonnie's finger for blood work, got some in the vial, capped it and took it to the lab at Hartselle Hospital. It wasn't an hour; she called to tell me she would be right back out to stick Bonnie again. The blood had clotted. She stuck Bonnie again and took it back to the lab. Forty-five minutes later the phone rang. Karen said, "Mrs. Summerford the blood clotted again, I'll be right out." Out she came again for more blood. This time she took it out of her arm. She told Bonnie that if it clotted this time, she would not be out anymore today. She would come tomorrow. She didn't want to stick her anymore today. I didn't hear from her anymore today, so I'm sure everything went okay.

I went to the ladies prayer meeting this morning. There were only five of us there. I pray that more would start coming. I know that prayer is the answer to everything. It is so easy to want to take things in our own hands and not pray about it.

This is the 11th day of August. I had called Kroger's for a refill on Bonnie's prescription. We began to bathe her but had to raise her head up some. The last few days it was harder for her to breathe when she was laid flat.

I was getting ready to go after her medicine at 2:00 p.m. I had already got some loving and I went into the kitchen for a minute. I heard Hope on the monitor saying, "Mrs. Summerford" real low. I went running into Bonnie's bedroom. She had been coughing some and trying to get strangled. Always before I could pat her, with my open hand, hard on her chest and she would be okay. This time I could tell she was worse.

I called Home Health and talked to Dauphy. As I was talking to her, right before my eyes I could see Bonnie getting bad. I told Dauphy I was calling the ambulance to take her to the hospital. I called the ambulance and told them she couldn't breathe well. They brought oxygen in with them and put it on her where she could breathe easier.

I called Jean; she came over to drive my car. She followed the ambulance to the hospital, parked and came in to be with us.

At first I didn't realize this would be the last trip that I would go with Bonnie to the hospital. I knew later, in my heart, she wasn't going to make it this time.

When we got to the emergency room they began to do tests on her. They took a chest x-ray to make sure she didn't have pneumonia. Bonnie began to aspirate and the nurse told me they were going to go down her nose and suction her out. I said, "Let her rest a minute." The nurse went to talk to the emergency room doctor. He told me if they didn't suction her out she was going to die. Of course I wanted them to suction. At first it came back into her mouth, but at last the nurses got it down her nose. They suctioned a bunch of stuff out with a good bit of phlegm. Dr. Vakaria was on call so he came to the emergency room after seeing Bonnie. He told me she had lost a lot of weight since the last time he had seen her. At first he told me they were moving her to the 3rd floor. After he talked to the emergency room doctor he came back in and said they were putting her in the Intensive Care Unit until maybe the next day. I believe that he knew she wasn't going to make it.

They moved her into the Intensive Care Unit and connected her up to the heart monitor. Betty Clemons was the emergency room nurse.

The therapist came up to suction her out again. She bled some in her throat. She gagged each time, but I knew it had to be done. Bonnie would look at me so helpless, like she was begging me for help. It broke my heart to see her in so much distress. All I could do was pray, which was the most important thing that could be done. Each time the nurse would suction I would love Bonnie, talk to her and pray for the Lord to help her.

Madeline came about 8:00 p.m. and stayed for awhile. During the time she was there Shirley had Wendell to call and check on Bonnie. At that few minutes she was better. I talked to Bonnie and she smiled at me. Needless to say, that was the last smile I would ever see on Bonnie upon this earth. After Madeline left, Bonnie began to get worse. The therapist did a breathing treatment and then suctioned her out. The last breathing treatment she did on Bonnie, she told me she didn't think it would help to suction her. There weren't any results coming back now. She asked me if I wanted her to go ahead and suction, and I told her, "No." One of her classmates, Sammie was on duty then. I looked at Sammie and said, "She's not going to make it this time." I knew it wasn't going to be long before the Lord called her home. Sammie looked at me. She came on duty 3rd shift. She had gone to school with Bonnie at Danville. She was Mike and Bonnie's nurse quite a few times when they were in the hospital.

I don't remember exactly what time it was, about 2:45 a.m., I told Sammie, "It's not going to be much longer." Bonnie was struggling so much to breathe and gasping as she did. They had the air conditioner on 66 and Bonnie was wringing wet with sweat. I would wipe it off with a wash cloth and it would be right back on her again. She had no fever; it was from struggling so to breathe.

Sammie came in and asked about my relatives and their phone numbers. A couple of nurses were there with us – a trainee and one from the 3rd floor. I gave Sammie the numbers and she began to call them. I knew it was getting down to the last little bit.

I was praying with Bonnie and telling her how much I loved her. It is so hard to watch one of your children in such distress; you want to breathe for them.

"Bonnie, it won't be long till you'll be crossing over. You'll see the Lord and Michael will also be there to greet you. Just remember that mother loves you. It won't be long till I see you again. The next time I see you and Mike, you both will be whole again." As I talked to her she opened her eyes half-way and looked as if she heard and understood what I was saying. "Lord, please take her on home," I said. It wasn't easy to beg the Lord to take Bonnie, like I had for Him to take Michael. But, I couldn't stand to see them suffer, gasping for breath. I loved my children with all my heart. This was my last one. This was all my family. Lord, please help me; give me the grace I need.

It was about 4:45 a.m. Madeline, Jean, T. C., Marie, and Brother Charles came in. Others had been called but couldn't come. Shirley was called but I knew she couldn't come, but would want to know. Hazel was called, I didn't know if she was able to come or not.

Bonnie would breathe a tiny bit, then it would seem like it would be a minute before she would breathe again. At 5:10 she took her last breathe. I knew she was in the presence of the Lord.

They called the emergency room doctor. It was Dr. Copley, the same doctor that was on duty when Mike was admitted when he passed away. She pronounced Bonnie dead. Oh my heart and down to the pit of my stomach hurt. A few minutes later Hazel and Kathy walked in. I was hoping she would see Bonnie before she passed away. The nurses told us to take all the time that we wanted to spend with her. When they took the C-pap off Bonnie, my precious baby was at peace. You could see it on her little face. We spent 45 minutes to an hour to say our good-byes to Bonnie.

After they called Peck, we stayed in there a few minutes. We then went into the hallway and sat, waiting on them to pick her up.

It brought back memories of Michael, with us sitting and waiting. It's so hard to watch them come and take your babies away. Nothing can compare to watching your babies pass away. But, I have the assurance of seeing them again one day. Thank you, Lord, for dying on the cross and making a way for each and every one of us – if we accept Christ as our Savior.

I had my car at the hospital because Jean had followed the ambulance and Dick picked her up late. As we began to leave Madeline asked me if I wanted to ride with her, I told her I would drive my car. She asked me if I was okay to drive, and I told her, "Yes." She said she was going to McDonald's to get us some biscuits.

As I arrived home and opened the door it was so quiet. I wanted to scream. I looked at the flashing light on the telephone. There were 25 messages. I began to make coffee because Madeline would be there soon. I made a few calls and it wasn't long till Madeline arrived.

We sat down at the table to eat. After praying, I tried to eat. The food seemed to get bigger the more I chewed. I knew I needed to eat because it had been a long time since I had eaten and there were lots of things to do.

Carleen and Jean came. Then Mike and Sandra came and took Bonnie's bed to put in their garage until after the funeral. I would have her casket where her bed was, like Mike's.

Carleen, bless her heart, swept and mopped. Madeline and Carleen dusted and straightened the house up. Jean helped us to move things around from under the carport.

People began to come over. Shirley, Wendell, and Tim came, and we just sat and talked.

I told Shirley, when Bonnie passed away, I could just see Michael motioning with his hands for Bonnie to come on in. Then, he looked at Bonnie and said, "Why didn't you bring Mom with you?" He always called me Mom and Bonnie would call me Mother.

After Shirley, Wendell, and Tim left we began to put stuff away. People began to bring in food. Frank and Sarah came, and then Fletcher. They all stayed a good while. I needed my family at a time like this, and they were there for me.

As people left and the house was quiet again I began to think, "Mike and Bonnie, what am I going to do now?" My precious angels are gone. Lord, I know that I'm going to have to depend entirely upon you. I'll have to depend on you to give me the strength and grace once more – this time to lay my beautiful angel in the grave. I already miss her so much. I tell her, "I go to check on you or get ready to do you feeding and then it comes to me, you're gone. I know you're in a better place, in the arms of our Heavenly Father. What better place could there be? You're with your Big Bubba now. I know you're happy. No more hurting or lying in that old hospital bed. But oh, how I miss you and Mike. You and Mike are what kept me going all these years. The Lord gave me the strength and faith, but having you and Mike in my life gave me the determination to do the things that needed to be done."

The Lord has answered my prayer. To be able to live and stay in good health to take care of Mike and Bonnie until the Lord called them home. He did that. There is no way I could ever be mad at the Lord for taking Mike and Bonnie on. Before they drew their last breath, I was begging the Lord to take them home. I couldn't stand to see them gasping for breath. It broke my heart. I loved them too much to see them suffer like that.

I slept fairly well last night. As I got up, the quietness was unreal. There was no TV on, and no Bonnie to whine because she didn't like a commercial being on. I looked over toward where Bonnie's bed was, no Bonnie, no bed. Sometimes for a split second, I think they're still here. Reality sets in and I know they're gone.

There are plenty of things to do today. After eating my breakfast, I got ready because Frank was to be here at 10:15, and he was right on time. On the way to Peck's I thought about how it has been less than a year since we made the first journey there. After the arrangements were made I gave the insurance policy to them and we left. We didn't have to go to the cemetery this time; they already knew where the gravesite would be.

We stopped at Wal-mart to get some things for Bonnie and things we would need at the house. Frank wouldn't let me pay for it. When we left, we headed for Decatur to look for an outfit to put on Bonnie. We were to meet Sarah there. I got a slip at J. C. Penney's because Wal-mart didn't have a white slip and all the rest were real short. Bonnie wore her clothes like a lady. No short dresses or skirts and no low-cut tops. I was so proud that Bonnie had convictions.

Frank went to look for clothes for himself, so Sarah and I started looking for clothes for Bonnie. We looked at J. C. Penney's while we were there. We also looked at Belk's, Sears, and a lot of other stores in the mall. They were either too short or too low-cut. The last store we went into was Bon Worth. I looked around and told the saleslady, "You have descent clothes." The other stores had clothes that appeal to the youth. When my eye caught the burgundy outfit, I knew Bonnie would have also approved of it. You can call us old fashioned, old foggy, or whatever, because I am. I can remember many, many years ago when I was lost. I would get in a chair, and turn up my hem just above my knees. Oh, the wasted years that I lived for the devil. Thank you Lord for showing me the way! Sarah wouldn't let me pay for the skirt and top. She said she was paying for it. What a blessing Frank and Sarah have been.

After we purchased the outfit we headed for the house. We hadn't eaten anything and it was way after lunch. We got something to eat and as Sarah and I were fixing to leave, Betty and Lois stopped by. I didn't get to visit with them as long as I would have liked to. We had to take the clothes to Peck's and go by Smith's to order flowers. Frank was staying at the house because people were bringing food by. I think he wanted to rest also, because he was having problems with his legs. We carried the clothes by Peck's then went to Smith's Florist to order the flowers. When we got there, I asked the lady if they would have time to do a blanket for the next day by 12:00. I told her my daughter had passed away and I was going to bring her home. She said yes. I picked out the flowers and she said, "These are for Bonnie Summerford." I looked at her and thought, I didn't tell her Bonnie's name. I got my purse open to pay and she said, "It's already been taken care of." I said, "What?" and she said it again. I asked her who paid for it and she said, "Jack and June Bailey." Isn't that just like the Lord? I told her I was beginning to think she might have ESP because I didn't tell her Bonnie's name. Sarah and I left and went back to the house. Patsy came up and was talking to Frank when we got home.

We sat around and talked for awhile, and then others began to come by. Quite a few came by that night to pay their respects and others brought food. We ate supper and sat and had fellowship. It is so sad that people don't visit one another until someone passes away. As we put things away people began to leave. Some offered to stay with me, but I wanted to be alone. Frank and Sarah asked me to go home with them. I really appreciated all the offers, but I just wanted to be at home and have time to think.

I went through the house, first to Mike's room and then to Bonnie's. I'm alone now, forever, till the Lord calls me home. I prayed, and then went to bed.

I had a fairly good night's sleep. I woke up a few times during the night. I would think about Mike and Bonnie, it would make me sad and my heart so heavy.

Morning finally came and I got up. I knew it wouldn't be long until people would start arriving. Then, it would be time for Peck's to bring Bonnie home. This visit, for her, would be like Mike's was. I should say my last visit with her earthly body.

I hurried to get a bath and dress before anyone arrived. I ate a little breakfast, but it is so hard to eat when a loved one passes away. Food is the last thing you think about.

Sometimes it seems like I hear Bonnie whine a little. I think that's not possible because my baby's gone. Is it wishful thinking? Maybe so; but, I know one day I'll see her again.

As people arrived some ate lunch, others just had something to drink. When we finished, the table was cleaned up and food put back in the refrigerator. People stood around and visited.

The florist brought flowers. Pallbearers came to help get her out of the hearse. I put Bonnie in her room, like I did with Michael. I didn't want either one in the living room. It wouldn't have seemed like the right thing, it seemed normal for them to be in their rooms.

As they opened the casket and fixed things, I went over. They stepped back and I looked at my second precious angel. Bubba was my big boy; I would tease him and call him Peanut. I would call Bonnie Little Tater Bug. As I looked at her face I could see bruises where the C-pap had made them around her little mouth and nose. Peck's tried to cover them up with make-up, but it still showed through. She looked just like she should say something. I know Mike and Bonnie are catching up on what has happened since they had seen each other last.

I could just hear Mike saying as Bonnie passed thru the Pearly Gates, "There's my sister." Oh, how they loved each other.

As I continued to look at Bonnie, tears ran down my face. Oh Lord, please help me. After Mike was born I was never by myself. Four years later Bonnie was born. We have always been together. My heart hurt so much from missing my Bonnie. It hurt so much when Mike passed away, but I still had Bonnie, so I had to go on. Leaning on Jesus, is what I have to do.

There were many friends, people from church, and family members that came by to pay their respects. Some wanted to stay with me and some wanted me to go home with them. I wanted to be home by myself with Bonnie. When all had left I went back to see Bonnie. "Mother loves you so much. I will miss you. You and Mike were my life," I told her. I know it will be the Lord that sees me through this. Thank you Lord for answering my prayer! Although it hurts, I'm thankful that you did allow me to live and stay in good health to take care of Mike and Bonnie. I know if I had passed away, before they did, there would have been nobody to take care of them. They would have had to go to a nursing home and I could not have died in peace.

Some people would think that I had lost my mind if they heard me talking to Bonnie. They would have thought the same about Mike. I always told them I loved them before I left or at bedtime after praying with them.

Roy and Eloise came by early. Brother Jack and June came while they were still here. We all talked awhile, and then they left. Martha, Hazel, and Carl came on out. Others began to come in. All the pallbearers were here when it was time for Peck to get Bonnie. The flowers were taken to be put in the van, all except the potted plants. Mike and Bonnie both had beautiful flowers that friends and family had sent.

I said my good-byes to Bonnie before they took her out to be put into the hearse. I knew from this day on it was going to be so different around here. No more TV on all the time and no loves and smooches from her like it was with Mike being gone. Even though I was so hurt from missing them both, I felt even closer to the Lord.

As they left with her my heart and the pit of my stomach felt so empty. We waited a little longer before we left to go to the church. I rode with Frank and Sarah like I did when Mike passed away. Mike's funeral was on a Saturday and Bonnie's was on a Sunday. It hasn't been a year since Mike passed away. Also, I lost my oldest brother April 29th of this year.

Are there sad farewells, yes, but one day there will be a glad reunion day. Mike and Bonnie are whole again. When my time comes I can hear the Lord say to Mike, "Here comes your mom." He will then turn to Bonnie and say, "Bonnie, here comes your mother." Boy, you talk about shouting; there will be a lot of that going on. We could sing "Glad Reunion Day."

As we arrived at the church, the parking lot was full, just like when Mike passed away. If we could see Mike he would have a big ole smile across his face. He would look at Bonnie and say, "I told you we were loved." They were an inspiration to me all these years. Mike was bedbound 18 years and Bonnie 17 years. The Lord was so good to us.

As we walked the isle to go to our seats I glanced at Bonnie. Later, I thought, Bonnie and Mike did get to go back to church one more time.

Steve, Ricky, and Ramona did the singing. Bonnie would have loved that. She always loved to hear them sing. The service started with Brother Jimmy Wright leading with prayer and saying a few things. Brother Wendell Callahan did the survivors. Then he began, "Let's pull back the curtains to Heaven and take a look – there's Moses" and he named others. Then he said, "There are Mike and Bonnie walking and talking with the Lord. Yes, I said walking and talking with the Lord." I couldn't help but cry. Although I knew they loved me, they wouldn't want to come back. I missed them so much and would love to hold them in my arms. They're in a better place than we are. After Brother Wendell was done, Brother Charles finished the service.

After people went around viewing Bonnie, they went back to their seats. I had told Peck Funeral Home I wanted to spend a few minutes with Bonnie. I wanted to with Mike, but I failed to tell them. They asked everyone to leave where I could be alone with Bonnie. As I went to the casket and looked at Bonnie, I began to tell her what a blessing she and Mike had been to me all these years. How much I loved her and missed her already. To look for me, because one of these days, and it might not be long, I would join them. I said my good-byes and gave my darling the last loving upon this earth.

I went out and got into the car with Frank and Sarah. Peck loaded Bonnie into the hearse and drove slowly toward Hartselle, escorted by the police. I thought as we rode toward the cemetery, this was another trip with the last of the two most precious jewels that I had in my life.

As we approached Mt. Tabor Cemetery, some that had left ahead of us were already there. As we parked and got out of our vehicles, my heart began to pound and my mouth was so dry. "Lord help me, you're going to have to give me grace again," I said. As we were seated Brother Charles stepped forward and began to speak. I can't remember what he said. I don't remember what he said with Mike, it just seems like my mind went blank; but, I was leaning on our precious Lord. As he finished and they shook our hands, we were ushered to our vehicles and began to drive away.

As we left the cemetery they began to lower Bonnie into the grave. My thoughts, first it was Mike and now it's Bonnie. Lord, they're in your loving care now. Thank you for all the years that you have given Mike and Bonnie to me to have - for they truly were mama's blessings.

> Amen, the Glory is to be given to the Lord.
> Edith Byrd Summerford

About the Author

EDITH IS THE MOTHER OF Mike and Bonnie Summerford and was their caregiver for more than 18 years. Some people may see the task of caring for two bed bound children as a burden. However, Edith saw this as a blessing. Edith resides in Hartselle, Alabama.

Edith Byrd Summerford
3456 Highway 36 West
Hartselle, AL 35640
256-773-0120

About The Book

*Y*ou've heard the old saying, "When life gives you lemons - make lemonade." Mama's Blessings will inspire you to make your lemonade. Trials and tribulations are part of our lives, and they appear when we least expect them. How we handle these situations depends on each individual, but by realizing if we rely on the Lord all things are possible. We must have the determination to make something good out of any situation that is beyond our control. Through faith, the Lord gives you strength and hope. Mama's Blessings is a testament to rely on the Lord through faith. I relied on the Lord, while caring for Mike and Bonnie, and He answered so many prayers and brought many blessings our way. Mike and Bonnie were truly "blessings" in my life.